BIRDS IN PERIL

BIRDS IN PERIL

By John P.S. Mackenzie

A guide to the endangered birds
of the United States and Canada

Illustrated by Terence Shortt

HOUGHTON MIFFLIN COMPANY, BOSTON 1977

This book is published in the United States by
Houghton Mifflin Company through special arrangement
with the publisher of origin, Pagurian Press Limited.

ISBN 0-395-25855-3

10 9 8 7 6 5 4 3 2 1

Printed and bound in Canada

for
Lois

Contents

Color Plates

Introduction

As an ethic and a concept of well-being for Canada and the United States, the environmental movement is almost completely the child of the twentieth century. During the last 75 years, we have progressed from a continent where words like ecology, habitat, and environment were unknown, to a time when they are keys to a crucial force, indeed to a movement affecting private and governmental decisions on every level, every day of our lives. And nowhere on earth are concerns for the environment so acute as in North America today.

It is perhaps strange, but also logical, that this is so. No continent has been so drastically altered by man in such a brief period of time. Our forefathers came upon a virtually unspoiled land less than four centuries ago. They and later arrivals viewed it as a wilderness to be conquered: to be tamed, altered, used, and exploited exclusively for the benefit of man. Forests were for timber, plains were for plowing, marshlands were for draining. Mammals, birds, fish, and reptiles were put here in bountiful supply by a benevolent deity for the use and enjoyment of people as needed—or simply at their whim. There seemed such an abundance of everything; it could never be used up.

But by the twentieth century, there were signs that it *could* be used up. The bison, the swans, the big game—all were disappearing. The passenger pigeon was gone; the Labrador duck was gone; the Carolina parakeet was gone. The lovely white egrets were fast disappearing; terns and other small birds by the thousands were being killed to decorate hats. North America was a slaughterhouse.

But voices were finally being raised. Out of the slaughter came the first of the Audubon Societies, and others of a protectionist mind. Public pressure produced the first protective legislation, and later came international treaties.

During the first 50 years thereafter, the emphasis was on protection: *thou shalt not kill a heron.* Now we are responding much more to the whole of the problem, as this book so admirably chronicles. Undreamed of only a few decades ago, our governments are now embarked on difficult and costly programs actually designed to preserve animals and plants of no economic value whatsoever — and nowhere has there been public outcry against these programs. The concept that every living species is a priceless heritage to be nurtured and preserved has finally, and at long last, come into its own.

Surely one of the most important reasons for this change of attitude and heart has been the cliff-hanging plight of species in particular peril: the California condor, whooping crane, Eskimo curlew, ivory-billed woodpecker, and the rest. These are now well-known public "heroes" of the environmental struggle. Even if we cannot save them, they will have served nobly in the cause: they will have educated and involved a generation or two in the environmental imperative. The author, John P.S. Mackenzie, has done us a service in bringing us up to date on the histories of birds in peril. Terence Shortt's beautiful paintings add visual grace to the pages that follow. The reader will take profit and pleasure from both.

ELVIS. J. STAHR
President, National Audubon Society
1977

Acknowledgments

Their protection cannot be urged.
Dr. C.G. Hewitt

This recommendation appeared in *The Conservation of Wildlife in Canada*, a book published in 1921 and written by Dr. C. Gordon Hewitt, the Dominion Entomologist and Consulting Biologist. The recommendation was made in a chapter headed "The Enemies of Wildlife" which discusses eagles, great horned owls, and "noxious hawks" — the goshawk, Cooper's, and the sharp-skinned as well as wolves and coyotes.

This form of prejudice, coming as it did from an eminent biologist, reflects the opinion of that time. Sadly, even today, hawks continue to be persecuted, although they have had legal protection for many years in both the United States and Canada. The goshawk, as an example, was then the most common hawk in many parts of its broad range, but now it is seldom seen.

Dr. Hewitt's book and other earlier studies aroused my curiosity about the misapprehensions which lead to predator control, bounty systems, and protective legislation. This, in turn, led to an increasing curiosity about the question of endangerment and extinction. I could find no work which summarized the current status of North American endangered birds. What follows is a result of my curiosity.

From the literature of the early part of the century, one senses that the various forms of wildlife were judged by their economic value. "Good" species were those which ate weed seeds and destroyed harmful insects; "bad" species were those which destroyed the "good." No one can deny the economic importance of birds to agriculture and forestry, but little attention was paid to the need for a natural balance between predator and prey. It has since been recognized that artificial imbalance can lead to overabundance of the protected species in terms of available food and space. It is, of course, still recognized that the control of some predators, such as coyotes, is necessary in heavily settled areas.

These questions are now much better understood by ecologists and biologists. Their views find expression in the interest of a better informed public, and in private and public organizations devoted to the study and protection of the ecology. Organizations such as the Audubon Society and the Nature Conservancy receive support and recognition as other than environmental freaks. Commercial interests such as mining, oil, gas, and forestry support environmental studies. Their community of interest is not always recognized by many academics who resist development almost automatically, because it is the only defence they know against exploitation. It is increasingly recognized, however, that a community of interest does exist, reducing the polarity of the positions and leading to common approaches to the same problem.

A striking example is the case of the proposed gas pipeline from the Mackenzie Delta to southern markets. The consortium of American and Canadian companies, which formed Canadian Arctic Gas Limited, has financed a multitude of environmental studies on all aspects of such a pipeline's impact on the perma-frost region (through which it will be built).

Today, governments recognize the need for research and protection. The United States Fish and Wildlife Service of the Department of the Interior and the Canadian Wildlife Service spend huge sums. They cooperate in planning and protection.

Without their assistance it would not have been possible for me to undertake the study of the twenty bird species which are described in the following pages.

The United States Fish and Wildlife Service in Washington provided me with a list of leaders of the various teams engaged in recovery of endangered species. Among those dedicated biologists who have given me much encouragement and advice concerning the species whose welfare is their responsibility, are:

Paul W. Sykes, Jr., Delray Beach, Florida (Florida Everglade kite); James L. Baker, Titusville, Florida (Dusky seaside sparrow); G. Vernon Byrd, Adak, Alaska (Aleutian Canada goose); Lovett E. Williams, Jr., Gainsville, Florida (Eastern brown pelican); Harold W. Werner, Homestead, Florida, (Cape Sable sparrow); David H. Ellis, Tucson, Arizona (Masked bobwhite quail); John Byelich, Lansing, Michigan and Jon C. Barlow, Toronto, Ontario (Kirtland's warbler); D.R. Johnston, Toronto, Ontario (Giant Canada goose); Val W. Lehmann, Kingsville, Texas (Attwater's greater prairie chicken); Sanford W. Wilbur, Ojai, California (California condor); Earl W. Godfrey, Ottawa, Ontario (Ipswich sparrow); and John P. Hubbard, Santa Fe, New Mexico (Mexican duck).

I am particularly indebted to the members of the library staff of the Royal Ontario Museum who permitted me full access to their shelves and directed me to valuable research papers. Judy Dick made this possible.

My friend, Terence Shortt, retired recently after forty-seven years in many capacities at the Royal Ontario Museum. Despite his wish for a release from the pressure of a full work load and the preparation of a book of his own, he graciously consented to paint a series of pictures to illustrate these pages. If this book has any lasting merit, it is through having encouraged Terry Shortt to create these beautiful drawings.

Valda Ondaatje has patiently and skillfully edited my draft material, besides making it fun.

Birds in Peril

Something more than death has happened, or, rather, a different kind of death. There is no survivor, there is no future, there is no life to be recreated in the form again. We are looking upon the uttermost finality which can be written, glimpsing the darkness which will not know another ray of light. We are in touch with the reality of extinction.
The Vineyard Gazette, April 21, 1933

The story of life is a constant progression of emergence, development, expansion, obsolescence, and, finally, extinction. The purpose of this book is to learn how the progression applies to birds, in particular North American birds on the brink of extinction, to answer why they are on the brink of extinction, and why these birds.

The first bird had reptilian features, a long, vertebrate tail, and lived 140 million years ago. In 1861, a slate splitter in Bavaria found a fossilized feather from this bird, *Archeopteryx lithographica*; the find confirmed the theory that feathers evolved from the enlarged scales of reptiles. Since *Archeopteryx* came and went, at least half a million more have come and gone: only a tiny fraction of the whole survives today (approximately 8,600 full species). The story of life is change, constant and unremitting; new species emerge, others fail.

THE IMPACT OF CLIMATE

In the past 140 million years, the earth has undergone countless changes: mountains and oceans have formed, great reptiles have evolved and passed on, climates have changed.

The Pleistocene period, which began two million years ago and ended ten thousand years ago, is the period of the ice ages; each age marked with distinct advances and withdrawals of arctic ice caps, each affecting plant and animal life on all but the earth's warmest regions. The last ten thousand years, in particular, have seen the emergence of many new species. As birds and other animals extend their range, they become isolated from the original group, and eventually develop their own characteristics. The strongest individuals produce the healthiest offspring, accentuating the differences from the original species. Thus, a new species emerges, capable of breeding only with its own kind. The new differs from the old, be it ever so slightly, in appearance, food preferences, and habitat requirements.

A good example is the herring gull. Ten thousand years ago, only one species of herring gull patrolled the existing seacoasts of the northern hemisphere. As more and more seacoasts appeared (because the ice melted) gulls spread to these new shores. Today, there are six full species — they have reinhabited each other's territory, but have retained their individual characteristics.

From this brief account, we can see that in recent geological times, *climate* has been the dominant factor in both the rise and fall of bird species. The present tiny breeding range of the Kirtland's warbler (page 159), for example, is due to climatic contraction, unique only because of the Kirtland's specific nesting requirements — pure stands of young jack pines growing in sandy soil. These conditions exist only in the northern peninsula of Michigan.

Drought may also make large areas uninhabitable. Recently, prolonged droughts in the northern part of Africa and in Brazil jeopardized even human occupation — the toll they took on wildlife cannot even be calculated.

THE IMPACT OF MAN

In recent historic times, however, man, not climate, has imposed the most impact on wildlife. Exploration and subsequent settlement in all parts of the world added a whole new dimension to the relatively small impact that native peoples had made on the same environment. The natives did, of course, make some: they killed for food and clothing. Their weapons, however, were primitive and inefficient. Even in affected or badly over-hunted areas enough breeding stock remained for species eventually to re-establish themselves. Many primitive people are nomadic — they move on when necessary; others live in areas where the animals they kill are migratory.

Seasonal burning by primitive people took its toll and still does. The Masai in East Africa, for example, regularly burn enormous areas of the Kenyan plains during the dry season to encourage grass and to discourage brush. But in general, primitive man's impact on his environment has been tolerable (except for some glaring exceptions on small islands where very specialized species developed that could exist nowhere else and could not take the pressure of constant overkilling).

Europeans have been the main culprits — they and the animals they introduced, knowingly or unknowingly, into new areas. Examples are legion. The mongoose was introduced to control snakes in Jamaica — the only problem was that after it had eaten the snakes, it turned to birds' eggs. Rats have been going ashore from European ships all over the world since the sixteenth century, causing devastation among many animal species. Goats in the Galapagos have virtually eliminated the food supply of the once-abundant giant tortoise. Modern man has been responsible for the elimination of much suitable habitat (by settlement) and outright slaughter (for food and skins). The available supply of fresh, clean water necessary to maintain life has been reduced; modern weapons have made killing easy; pesticides have increased pollution many fold.

THE DODO

The dodo is a tragic example of man's impact. This flightless and helpless bird has become a synonym for extinction, but it was only one of twenty-five bird species to disappear forever from the Mascarenes. These islands, Mauritius, Réunion, and Rodriguez, are found some four hundred miles east of Madagascar in the Indian Ocean. They range in size from 970 square miles (Réunion) to forty-three square miles (Rodriguez). The islands are spectacularly beautiful, and, although discovered as early as 1505, were not permanently settled until the seventeenth century. They then became a source of food and fresh water to the trading ships plying the eastern route.

At the time of settlement, there were forty-one species of endemic birds on the islands, of which some, including the dodo, had become highly specialized. Of the original forty-one, twenty-five are now extinct.

The dodo was an ungainly and supremely ugly bird. It weighed about fifty pounds and was taken for food in large numbers. Because it nested on the ground, rats, dogs, and cats, (all introduced) could easily take its eggs, and did. By 1680, the dodo had disappeared from Mauritius; by 1800, the last of an associated form had disappeared from Rodriguez.

This ugly story is typical of many such stories and it is just one example of man's thoughtless slaughter and of depredation by rats and domestic animals gone wild.

THE GREAT AUK

The great auk suffered a similar fate — only in a different setting. The last pair was killed off the coast of Iceland on June 3, 1844, but by this time it had been gone from the British Isles for ten years and from its breeding colonies (from New England to Ireland) for years before that.

The bird's widespread breeding range protected it from sudden natural catastrophe, but its inability to fly, coupled with its apparent lack of fear of humans, assured its doom. Wide-ranging fishermen and their firearms did their work — the great auk could not survive this pressure and succumbed.

THE HEATH HEN

Nor could the hapless heath hen tolerate the combined onslaught of civilization and shotguns. Originally, the heath hen flourished in open brushy country from Massachusetts to Virginia. Early settlers practically made it a staple of their diet. As the forests were cleared, more nesting and feeding areas were created — one would think to the heath hen's advantage. Unfortunately, it also kept it within range of the farmer's shotgun.

By the middle of the nineteenth century, the heath hen had been extirpated from the United States mainland, but a small colony remained on Martha's Vineyard, off the Massachusetts coast. Here, protected by law but not entirely by custom, it slowly increased — from two hundred in 1900 to two thousand in 1916. That year the heath hen's habitat was burned in a disastrous fire: disastrous because the heath hen never recovered. The last specimen was seen on March 11, 1932. On April 21, 1933, a long editorial appeared in *The Vineyard Gazette*, lamenting its passing. An excerpt appears at the beginning of this chapter and sums up finality in a dramatic way.

THE PASSENGER PIGEON

Another case involves the passenger pigeon. Early descriptions of vast flocks which "darkened the sky" on migration are today difficult to believe. In 1806, Alexander Wilson, the great ornithologist, estimated one flock to contain more than two billion birds! The flock represented probably one half of the total population. Audubon was traveling in Kentucky, from Henderson to Louisville, in the autumn of 1813, when "the light of the noon day sun was obscured as by an eclipse" — by a migrating flock of passenger pigeons. He calculates that a flock one mile wide, passing at sixty miles an hour, would, in three hours, account for 1,115,136,000 birds, and "the quantity (of food) necessary for supplying this vast multitude must be 8,712,000 bushels per day."

The flock took three days to pass.

He writes, too, of the vast numbers shot and killed while roosting at night, the wagonloads carted away, the three hundred hogs that were driven a hundred miles to fatten on the carcasses, and comments, "Persons unacquainted with these birds might naturally conclude that such dreadful havoc would soon put an end to the species. But I have satisfied myself, by long observation, that nothing but the gradual diminution of our forests can accomplish their decrease, as they not infrequently quadruple their numbers yearly, and always at least double it." How wrong he was!

Audubon overestimated the number of nesting colonies, but one appraisal of 138 million birds in a single nesting group (in Wisconsin) is considered reliable. The deciduous forests, on which these flocks relied for food and nest sites, were fast being cut down to make way for farms, and there was simply not enough food to go around. But not all passenger pigeons nested in large flocks. Some nested in small colonies. Therefore it is possible the species might have survived had it not been so indiscriminately slaughtered.

But the destruction at nesting sites and roosts was enormous; carloads were shipped to urban markets each fall. Because each female laid only one egg (a few may have laid two), and because she would not nest again that year if disturbed, made the decline, when it finally came, catastrophic. By 1870, the only flocks left were those close to the Great Lakes. In 1899, the last wild bird was shot; on September 1, 1914, the last passenger pigeon died in the Cincinnati Zoo. Sic transit gloria!

The dodo, great auk, heath hen, and passenger pigeon cannot be brought back to life — for them it is too late. But for the thirty-two on today's endangered list, there is still hope, albeit in some cases, a very slim one. Fifty California condors, ninety-nine whooping cranes, the occasional Eskimo curlew, the almost-gone ivory-billed woodpecker — can we save them? First, let us look at their enemies.

DDT

At this point, it is tempting to add to the emotional outpourings of the last twenty-five years and denounce DDT and other associated poisons. That, however, has already been done all too well (the late Rachel Carson's eloquent book *The Silent Spring* was one of the first). DDT's chain reaction, starting in soil and in algae, through mammals to the final consumer (the raptor and fish eater) is now understood all too well. As a result, pelicans, eagles, and falcons are in danger.

In 1971, the agricultural use of DDT was banned in Canada; in the United States it was banned in 1972. Despite the ban, in 1974, the Environmental Protection Agency of the United States government permitted DDT to be sprayed over 420,000 acres in Oregon, Washington, and Idaho to combat the Douglas fir tussock moth. (Reports of widespread losses of birds have not yet been confirmed.)

Nor is it better north of the border. At this moment, there is mounting pressure to resume DDT spraying to combat the spruce budworm in eastern Canada.

Although in general the environment is improving, it will be years before all the affected species recover. What happens is this: shells of eggs laid by birds carrying DDE (a residue of DDT) become very thin as a result of the chemical build-up in the bird's system. Thinning makes the egg incapable of bearing the weight of the brooding parent — and it breaks. (Even if they do not break, DDE-contaminated eggs are often infertile.)

In South America, where many of our birds winter, DDT is still commonly used. The Arctic peregrine falcon, for example, feeds there on contaminated prey; neither is it safe in the summer in the north, for its summer prey may well be carrying poison from its wintering area. DDT is not the only culprit. Other potentially dangerous pesticides are still in use.

OTHER POLLUTANTS

Other forms of pollution, real and threatened, are with us. In the arctic, off-shore drilling continually presents the possibility of leaks and blowouts — if oil were to spread under arctic ice, the effects would be far-reaching and long-lasting. All over the world, increased tanker traffic results in more and more oil spills, devastating our fishing grounds and beaches. In the west, oil traffic will increase many fold when the pipeline from Prudoe Bay to Valdez, Alaska, is completed, shipping oil by sea from Alaska to west coast ports. Chemical spills into rivers, lakes, and along the coasts occur almost daily. (Chemical pollution of the Mississippi near its mouth has been responsible for the deaths of half the birds in a struggling brown pelican colony.)

RATE OF EXTINCTION

Lists of extinct species generally start from the year 1600, which coincides with wide-scale European exploration and settlement. Historically, island and shore-nesting species have been the most vulnerable. While facts are obscure and opinions conflicting, the International Council for Bird Preservation (associated with the International Union for Conservation of Nature and Natural Resources), lists 165 species and subspecies as having disappeared since 1600. Of these, 105 species are well documented, mostly through museum specimens; about twenty are known from bones and from somewhat fanciful, unprofessional descriptions; the balance from tales and drawings of early travelers (as these are mostly from untrained observers, they are classified as hypothetical). What does emerge, however, is the constant alarming rate of increase in the number of extinctions.

I.U.C.N. Tabulation of Extinctions

Period	Number of Extinctions (species and subspecies)
1600-1700	16
1701-1800	22
1801-1900	79
1901-1975	48
	total 165

By another measure it may be calculated that since 1600, seventy-six full species have disappeared. Directly or indirectly, almost all have been caused by man: thirteen because of hunting, eleven because of introduced domestic animals and rats, fourteen because of habitat destruction through tree felling, marsh draining, and agriculture, and the rest lost to the pressure of new bird species introduced into their habitat.

SPECIES IN PERIL

In North America, the United States Fish and Wildlife Service, an arm of the Department of the Interior of the United States Government, determines which species are to be classified as endangered; and establishes programs for their recovery. (The Service is responsible for the whole of the continental United States, Hawaii, and Puerto Rico.)

At present, the list contains the following numbers of endangered species:

- Fifty-five species of fish, including ten trout and one pike.
- Nineteen species of reptiles, including both the alligator and the crocodile.
- Forty-three species of mammals, including five bats, eight whales, four wolves, four seals, two deer, the grizzly and glacier bears, the eastern cougar, and three mountain sheep.
- Seventy species and subspecies of birds: thirty-one Hawaiian, seven Puerto Rican, thirty-two continental North American.

It is the thirty-two bird species and subspecies that spend part or all of the year in the continental United States and in Canada that concern us here. They are:

Eastern brown pelican
California brown pelican
Florida great white heron
Aleutian Canada goose
Tule white-fronted goose
Mexican duck
California condor
Florida Everglade kite
Southern bald eagle
Prairie falcon

American peregrine falcon
Arctic peregrine falcon
Northern greater prairie chicken
Lesser prairie chicken
Attwater's prairie chicken
Masked bobwhite quail
Whooping crane
Florida sandhill crane
Mississippi sandhill crane
California clapper rail
Light-footed clapper rail
Yuma clapper rail
California black rail
Eskimo curlew
California least tern
Red-cockaded woodpecker
American ivory-billed woodpecker
Bachman's warbler
Golden-cheeked warbler
Ipswich sparrow
Dusky seaside sparrow
Cape Sable sparrow

Not only are the birds on the official list in peril. New birds are constantly under consideration for listing; others are removed from the list. Removal from the list means one of three things — the species has made a comeback and is no longer considered endangered, its earlier status was misunderstood, or, it has become extinct. The Smyrna seaside sparrow (a subspecies of the seaside sparrow family), which never made the endangered species list, formerly lived and bred between New Smyrna and Amelia Island on Florida's east coast. Urban sprawl so reduced its habitat that it is now probably extinct — in recent years not one has been seen. Had people realized in what dire straits it was, steps could perhaps have been taken to save it. In all probability the Smyrna is not the only one; many more species may be disappearing, with nobody the wiser.

Other species which were once in serious trouble, or thought to be, are now in reasonable condition — the giant Canada goose, the trumpeter swan, and the Hudsonian godwit are cases in point. Their stories have been included in this book (pages 55, 37, and 137) to show that intelligent research and dedicated conservation efforts *can* turn the tide.

Decades of over-shooting and ever-increasing constriction of habitat almost finished the trumpeter swan, with the result that by the early 1930s, only sixty-nine were left south of the Canadian border. (It was not known then that an independent population of several thousand still existed in the interior of British Columbia and Alaska.) In 1939, the United States Fish and Wildlife Service began an all-out effort to save the trumpeter swan. Eventually, it did. (See page 37.)

The giant Canada goose has only been recognized in the last fifteen years as a subspecies of the Canada goose; consequently its numbers and range have been little understood. Confusion with the western Canada goose, together with bureaucratic obstinacy, delayed not only recognition, but, more importantly, rehabilitation efforts. A few years ago when finally the subspecies was recognized as such, many experts thought it was already extinct. In the United States it *was* almost extinct; in the Canadian prairies, however, it still hung on. (See page 55.)

Only one bird on today's endangered list has not been brought to its present desperate state because of man — the Bachman's warbler (page 153). It has probably reached the end of existence on its own. And only the Eskimo curlew's plight can be blamed on over-shooting. The others are in peril because of human interference of another kind — slaughter, constriction of habitat, or poisons introduced into their habitat.

WHAT IS BEING DONE?

When and how does a bird get on the Endangered Species List and what good does it do? Under the terms of the Endangered Species Act of 1973 (as well as other legislation before 1973), the United States Fish and Wildlife Service of the Department of the Interior is responsible for recognizing endangered species and for dealing with the problem. Getting a bird on the list is a long, tedious process involving much red tape and bureaucratic paper shuffling; deliberately so (perhaps) to avoid frivolous and self-interested claims from unqualified groups.

The process begins with an application from a private, state, or federal body (or from the Service itself). Next, interested agencies are notified and consulted, environmental and impact assessments are made, a draft of a recovery plan is made, and funds to finance the project are found.

After a species has been officially listed, a team of specialists is appointed to take charge of the project. They map out a specialized recovery plan, which may take up to a year or more to complete. (On page 34 we have included the outline of a draft recovery plan.) When the plan is complete, it is presented to the Fish and Wildlife Service for amendment, approval, or rejection.

If accepted, the plan goes into action, with a leader, a budget, and the power to act. The recovery team is totally in charge until, hopefully, the species has recovered to the point that it needs no more special treatment. In the case of some species, such as the Eskimo curlew and the ivory-billed woodpecker, it is pointless to take remedial action: it is too late.

The program has its flaws. Only six full-time scientists are on staff at the Fish and Wildlife Service to list all plants and animals — and they simply cannot keep up with the work. From time to time, the Service has been pressured by conservation groups and other emotionally involved groups to give special attention to the glamor species, while others, more in need of help, are put aside. The Smyrna seaside sparrow is a case in point. Conflicts have developed, not only among the myriad of interested parties — academics, government scientists, and the partially informed, but also among untrained conservation groups, wildlife managers, and state and federal agencies. Politicians are often caught in the middle.

There are other problems. Researchers have to give thirty days public notice for much of their direct contact with each endangered species, thus hampering and delaying their work. Some research tools, for example banding and monitoring, are still causing controversy and bickering.

Despite these problems, much good work is being done. Enormous sums are being spent — on acquiring new habitat, on research, on land and marsh improvement, on propagation. In comparison with the lethargy of earlier years public interest is high, and, where previously the profit principle reigned supreme, today the environment sometimes has a chance.

In this book we have not attempted to describe at length all the species which are officially listed as endangered. Most of the others are in danger because of loss or degradation of their habitat: the Florida great white heron, the four rail subspecies (whose marshes are disappearing), the red cockaded wood-pecker, and the golden-cheeked warbler, for example. The California brown pelican's story is combined with the eastern brown pelican's. Attwater's greater prairie chicken has been selected for inclusion because of its limited range; hence more is known about it than about either the northern greater prairie chicken or the lesser prairie chicken. They, however, face the same problems — in a different locale. The Florida sandhill crane, a subspecies of the greater sandhill crane, is resident in Alabama, Mississippi, southern Georgia, and Florida. It has been much reduced because of overshooting and egg-collecting; also because of predation by raccoons, snakes, and crocodiles. It still numbers some two to three thousand individuals and is not in imminent danger.

Eastern Brown Pelican

(Pelecanus occidentalis carolinesis)

There are two pelican species in North America — the white and the brown. The white pelican (*Pelecanus erythrorhynchos*) is the larger of the two. It has a wingspan of nine feet and a length of over four feet, an enormous orange bill (gray in immatures), and a pure white body except for the black flight feathers. It nests in the interior, on lakes in forests and plains, from California to northern Alberta. Nests, almost invariably on islands, are scooped in the ground. The white pelican is a migratory bird and is not endangered. In the fall it heads south — from the southern United States to Guatemala.

The brown pelican is non-migratory. It nests on coastal islands on both coasts of North and South America. It has a wingspan of about seven feet and a weight of up to eight pounds. The brown does not have the dashing appearance of the white. It is mostly brown-gray, with a white neck in winter and a chestnut-colored neck in summer. It has a yellow crown, dark bill, and dark pouch. In North America two subspecies exist — the western California brown pelican (*Pelecanus occidentalis californicus*) and the eastern brown pelican (*Pelecanus occidentalis carolinesis*). It is the eastern brown pelican that concerns us here. It once bred from eastern Mexico around the Gulf, off Texas, Louisiana, and Florida, to the Atlantic coast off North Carolina. Today, only the Florida population is thriving. Man and pesticides have caused its decline.

The brown pelican dives for fish, usually from thirty feet or more, folding its wings almost straight back as it hits the water. The fish is temporarily stunned by the impact. The pelican seizes this opportunity, opens its bill, and takes the fish, along with some sea water. It pops back to the surface and expels the water from its pouch, transferring the fish to its gullet. Brown pelicans seldom leave salt water. They prefer to fish along the coast but occasionally they are seen as far as thirty miles from shore.

Almost invariably, pelicans build their nests in colonies — among mangroves, in low bushes, or on low-lying bars where the nests are scratched into the surface. Normally, three eggs are laid. The hatchlings are bald, and, to survive, must be constantly protected from sun and rain until the down has grown.

THE DECLINE

Although no one knows the extent of early colonies, brown pelicans were abundant until the late 1930s. In 1931, the Louisiana population was 75,000 to 85,000; in 1938, it was 10,000 breeding birds — (more, of course, if immatures are included). By 1961, two hundred pairs were left. They produced a hundred nestlings. In 1962, only six pelicans were found, and none thereafter. Where there had been large colonies in Texas, only four nests were found in 1967; two in 1968. In the Carolinas, the same situation existed — the pelican population declined rapidly. On the credit side, Florida numbers have remained stable. Since 1966, aerial surveys have sighted between six and seven thousand nests every year and the total number of pelicans here is about 30,000.

Pelican colonies are subject to rapid and significant fluctuation — hurricanes, food shortages, predation, and human vandalism take their toll; development devastates other colonies. The Louisiana experience is the most drastic. Between 1950 and 1962, the brown pelican disappeared entirely. Ironically, it is Louisiana's official bird.

Why has the brown pelican vanished so quickly from Louisiana, Texas, California, and the Carolinas? Why is it still holding its own in Florida? The answer is chemical poisoning of fish by DDE (a residue of DDT). The contaminated fish is eaten by the pelican, whose eggs are, in turn, contaminated. Thin eggshells result. Eggs containing more than 2.5 parts per million of DDE simply do not hatch — they break under the weight of the brooding bird. The 2.5-parts-per-million critical level is lower than for other fish-eating birds; hence the pelican is the most susceptible to DDE poisoning, a fact obvious from the statistics. During the 1960s, the level of contamination was so high in the Mississippi River, massive fish die-offs occurred. In California, ocean waters around the pelican colony on Anacapa Island were polluted by discharge from Montrose Chemical Corporation's plant in Los Angeles, a manufacturer of DDT. Finally, only a lawsuit could stop the discharge. Eggs in the Florida colonies have never reached the critical contamination level, and it is the brown pelican's broad dispersion that has saved it from extinction. Had the entire population lived in Louisiana, the bird would be extinct. The Florida population is the only one capable of survival; a catastrophe here would be fatal.

WHAT IS BEING DONE?

In January, 1968, a plan to save the eastern brown pelican emerged from a meeting promoted by the National Audubon Society and the Louisiana Wildlife and Fisheries Commission. Thirty biologists and wildlife managers from various states and from federal and private agencies decided to act. First, they established the "Brown Pelican Newsletter" for the information of interested biologists. Second, they started a program of public information. Third, they coordinated a banding program and decided to census the brown pelican population in each relevant area.

As a result of the conference, the eastern brown pelican was placed on the endangered species list in 1970, and a program to stock the former colonies in Louisiana with young birds from Florida was implemented. The first fifty birds were transplanted to Grand Terre Island in the summer of 1968 and more subsequently, until 765 had been moved by 1976. The story has a mixed ending: nesting at Grand Terre has been successful, but in the spring of 1975 many pelicans, both white and brown, died as a result of heavy pollution, reducing the colony

from four hundred to two hundred and fifty. A few were sent to the Rockefeller Wildlife Refuge, but they failed.

Since 1972, when the use of DDT was banned in the United States, nesting success has improved dramatically, both in California and in Louisiana. DDE levels in eggs have declined quickly, raising hopes that continued bird transplants to former nesting sites are not in vain.

In September, 1975, under the terms of the Endangered Species Act, the United States Fish and Wildlife Service appointed a recovery team. The team consists of seven members, led by Lovett E. Williams, Jr., a biologist with the Florida Game and Fresh Water Commission. The preliminary draft of the recovery plan, released in November, 1976, is still subject to review and approval. The plan states: "A recovery plan is a guide to show how the species or population might be brought back from near extinction. Hopefully, its successful implementation would result in the species being removed entirely from the endangered list." The plan identifies the problems and proposes solutions. Its cost will be $269,000 (to the end of 1979). The objective is to prevent extirpation of the eastern brown pelican in any portion of its range by maintaining natural and restored colonies and by natural reproduction. The plan involves the following steps:

- Record locations of all nesting sites used since 1950.
- Characterize suitable nesting habitat. Determine why some places are used for nesting, others not.
- Develop methods to correct site deficiencies.
- Select sites to be stocked and prepare stocking plans with the cooperation of federal and state agencies.
- Develop stocking methods. Test, evaluate, and improve present procedures for capturing, transporting, and releasing pelicans; examine and evaluate alternatives to using wild pelicans. (Louisiana and Texas are the states to be stocked.)

- Find new sources of stock, establishing criteria to ensure that existing wild stock is not endangered.
- Monitor new colonies for extent of reproduction and pollution.
- Determine theoretical and existing stumbling blocks, for example, chemical contamination resulting in egg thinning or in death; water quality; danger from oil or chemical spills; human interference (resulting in nest desertion); interference from predators; erosion and plant cycles; disease; food supply.
- Measure pesticide contamination.
- Maintain regular inventories of populations, their distribution and their productivity.

The recovery plan outlines other measures. Two visits yearly are to be made to each colony to band several hundred young birds. The delicate subject of taking healthy specimens is broached, with a provision that injured, sick, and dead birds are to be made available to museums. Captive rearing of brown pelicans is to be encouraged to maintain breeding stock in case of catastrophe to the wild population; to provide stock for research; and to supply birds for public viewing. Crippled birds are to be kept captive and are to be encouraged to reproduce.

The plan recognizes the importance of public support and hopes to get it by providing accurate, timely news releases, pamphlets, and signs at fishing docks. Not only pollution, but habitat disturbance is a major cause of nesting failure, and the public is less likely to interfere with pelican colonies if it is properly informed. Of course, game laws must be enforced. The statement "Section 7 of the Endangered Species Act of 1973 should be strictly enforced by the U. S. Fish and Wildlife Service to make maximum use of the provision in the Act that would prevent any federal agency from becoming involved in any activity that would degrade the critical habitat of the brown pelican," contains a veiled warning to other government agencies that changing the use of lands already under federal ownership must not be permitted.

THE FUTURE

Since 1950, forty-five colonies are known to have been occupied — twenty-six on state-owned, nine on federally owned, and ten on privately owned island marshes. Whether state and privately owned lands are safe refuges is debatable; ideally all colonies should be brought into federal refuges or into other, well-protected areas.

In Louisiana, Texas, and the Carolinas, the plan's provisions to detect changes in reproduction, egg quality, egg shell thickness, pollution of the habitat, and food quality are particularly important. In Florida, while the population remains stable, they are less so.

The immediate goal? To stabilize the population in the Carolinas at or above its present levels, and to restore all former colonies in Texas and Louisiana to at least two hundred pairs. Successful implementation will take several years, but because pesticide pollution is on the decline, there is hope.

Trumpeter Swan

(Olor buccinator)

The original purpose of this book was to write only about the endangered species — species officially listed as endangered by the United States Fish and Wildlife Service and by the International Council for Bird Preservation. On a number of counts, however, we cannot resist including the trumpeter swan. It was listed as endangered for many years, but is no longer. Its recovery — from a low of sixty-nine birds in 1932 to a stable level of more than seven hundred in the western United States alone — is due entirely to a dedicated group of government biologists and conservationists. The trumpeter is included here to illustrate how close a species can come to extinction and still recover.

Besides the seven hundred trumpeters in the west, a breeding population of about four thousand has been identified in British Columbia and Alaska. The trumpeter's brush with destiny and its narrow escape make an interesting study; let us begin at the beginning.

HISTORY AND APPEARANCE

There are eight species of swans in the world of which two, the trumpeter (*Olor buccinator*) and the whistling swan (*Olor columbianus*), are native to North America. The mute swan (*Cyg-*

nus olor) was introduced from Europe many years ago. Today, a small population of wild mute swans lives on the east coast of America. (The mute is also the swan most often seen in parks and zoos.)

The trumpeter is the world's largest swan. Adult birds are all white, although the head and neck may be stained from ferrous water while feeding. The bill and legs are black or dark gray. The wingspan of the male is eight feet; compared with about six feet for the female. Length is about five feet. Weights vary considerably, but twenty-seven to twenty-eight-pound males are not uncommon; females weigh about five pounds less. Immature birds resemble adults, except they are brownish-gray. The bill is pink, becoming darker after one year.

Trumpeter and whistling swans are so alike that visual differentiation is almost impossible unless one can see the whistler's yellow or orange patch at the base of its bill. The patch, however, cannot be seen more than fifty feet away. The voice is the key: the trumpeter is well named. As W.E. Banko observes in his book, *The Trumpeter Swan*, published in 1960, "The call has a definite hornlike quality over a wide vocal range and may be uttered from one to a number of times at widely spaced intervals or in staccato fashion. The trumpeter gives voice perhaps most often in flight, but also commonly while on land or floating on water."

The trumpet call can be heard more than a mile away. The whistler also is aptly named — its cry is a whistling *wow, wow, wow* sound, louder at the end.

Early records of the nesting and wintering range of the trumpeter have been pieced together by Banko. Using archeological data and early journals as his sources, Banko has established that the nesting range extended from Alaska, across the Northwest Territories, to central Hudson Bay, around James Bay, south through the Great Lakes, and westward across the central and northwestern states. The bird's winter range included the Mississippi Valley, around the Texas coast, and the Atlantic coast south from New Jersey to the Carolinas.

How populous was the trumpeter when settlers first came to North America? No one knows exactly, but it must have been fairly common. In 1709, an account from North Carolina refers to "great flocks in the winter," and in 1795, Samuel Hearne, of Hudson Bay Company fame, writes that great numbers were taken by the Indians; not only for food, but also for feathers. Evidence unearthed from Indian kitchen-middens supports his statement — long before the first Europeans arrived, Indians took large numbers of swans.

Early settlers also used swans extensively for food, as the following eighteenth century comment illustrates: "A Cygnet, that is a last year's Swan, is accounted a delicate dish, as indeed it is. They are known by their Head and Feathers, which are not so white as the Old ones."

THE DECLINE

Starting about 1770 and continuing until 1903, swan skins were brought and sold in the market place. For example, 5,072 skins were sold in London in April, 1828; later that year four thousand more were shipped from the Northwest Territories. Although no record has been kept of how many trumpeters and how many whistlers were killed, the trumpeter was the principal victim.

The numbers shipped gradually declined — from thousands to hundreds. By 1890, only a very few were sent to England, and for a very good reason: there were very few left to send. Mr. Banko concludes that "the effect of such exploitation on the far-flung breeding populations of this species for more than a hundred and twenty-five years must have been devastating and largely responsible for its extermination over vast regions, particularly in the heart of its Canadian breeding range."

Remember, too, that the egg-collecting craze was then at its height. The swan's scarcity is obvious when we look at the price of its eggs — in 1892, trumpeter eggs cost $4.00; whooping crane eggs $3.00; the heath hen's $3.00. (The heath hen is now extinct.)

The trumpeter could not take this sort of pressure. By the end of the nineteenth century, it had vanished from North Dakota, Nebraska, Minnesota, Iowa, Missouri, Wisconsin, and Indiana. It is true that the breeding population south of the 49th Parallel was never large, and suitable range was limited; still, man was chiefly to blame for the swan's decline.

In Washington, it survived for a few more years. In 1932, the last remnant — sixty-nine birds — remained where Wyoming, Montana, and Idaho meet, and it was in this high plateau region that successful recovery took place.

Trumpeter swan ▶

TMShortt.

RECOVERY

By the early 1930s, the outlook was gloomy. The few remaining birds nested only in the Centennial Valley in southwestern Montana and in the vicinity of Yellowstone National Park in Wyoming. In 1935, hoping to save the species from extinction, the United States Government acquired approximately 13,000 acres of the Centennial Valley. The area became the Red Rock Lakes Migratory Waterfowl Refuge. It includes Upper and Lower Red Rock Lakes and a myriad of ponds and marshes. It is ideal habitat for the trumpeter, containing virtually everything the bird needs — stable, shallow water; drier patches for nesting; a reliable food supply; and a remote environment. The valley, at an elevation of 6,600 feet, lies between two mountain ranges. It has a gentle gradient, little erosion, clear water, and a remarkably abundant growth of aquatic plants.

Some fifty miles to the east, in Wyoming, the Yellowstone National Park provides a different habitat — not as suitable as the Red Rock's. Here are many glacial lakes at different elevations. Most lakes are treelined and have relatively small marsh areas; quite different from the continuous marsh and shallow lakes of Red Rock, and not one of the lakes in Yellowstone supports more than one pair of trumpeters during the nesting season.

The swan population in both areas is essentially nonmigratory, although in winter most birds move out of the Red Rocks Lake Refuge. The refuge contains a number of warm springs around which the water has been impounded. Part of the flock comes here in the winter. This ice-free area cannot, however, support the main flock during very cold weather. It cannot even support the few swans who come here to winter — there is not enough food. The solution? Grain is supplied regularly by the refuge personnel to supplement natural food supplies. Although artificial feeding as a management technique is deplored, it is considered necessary in this case.

Most of the flock moves to the main winter feeding area outside the refuge on Henry's Fork of the Snake River, some thirty miles south of the main breeding area. Here, several miles of river are kept open by the warm springs which supply it, even in the coldest weather. A few miles to the east, warm water from the Yellowstone's geysers keeps many more miles of river open. These rivers are shallow and suitable for swans and other up-ending waterfowl (waterfowl who feed on the bottom while still floating on the surface). Also, these streams meander through open meadow country. The advantages of open meadows are twofold: swans have plenty of room to take off, and predators cannot hide in open areas.

The combination of good nesting and good winter habitat in a small area has undoubtedly been responsible for this swan population's survival. If, in winter, it had to make long migratory flights in search of food, it could not have survived. Another advantage is that this area, at the corners of northeastern Idaho, northwestern Wyoming, and southern Montana, has been only sparsely populated by a few ranchers. There is little hunting pressure. Although some birds have been shot and others shipped alive to zoos, by and large, man has been benevolent.

LIFE CYCLE

For a month or more before the spring break-up, trumpeters fly from their feeding areas to spend part of the day on the frozen marshes where they will later nest. Here they display the territorial aggression typical of the nesting period: strange birds are driven off with posturing or with trumpeting, and are even attacked. The amount of territory claimed by each pair varies greatly. It appears to depend on the nature of the marsh itself — whether it be islands or shoreline — also on the food supply. Captive birds are satisfied with very little space of their own; wild trumpeters require from seventy to one hundred and fifty acres per pair.

Most nests are built on muskrat houses and are used year after year. Made entirely of vegetable material gathered in the immediate vicinity, the nest is built by both the cob (male) and the pen (female). It is made on top of a foundation of coarser material. Long after the eggs have hatched, it is a strong focal point in the early lives of the cygnets — during the day for resting and at night for brooding. When the time comes to leave the nest, it is an unrecognizable mess of shell, feathers, and defecation.

A thorough study of the wild trumpeter's nesting, egg-laying, incubating, and hatching habits is difficult to make because of the bird's tendency to desert when disturbed. We do know, however, that five or six eggs are laid, and that incubation lasts about thirty-three days, with the female doing all the incubating. Most years cygnets are hatched by the end of June. In the years when hatching, because of bad weather, is delayed until mid-July, the young are usually trapped by autumn frost before they can fly. Unlike small passerine birds (birds with feet adapted for perching), which within a short time grow to the size of their parents and learn to fly, swans do not fly until they are about four months old. Since freeze-up is about the end of October, the hatching date is crucial.

During the summer, cygnets grow from about seven ounces when hatched to about fifteen pounds. They feed on a mixture of plant and animal food, switching gradually from a ninety-five percent animal diet in the first few weeks to a full diet of plants.

Nesting success is vital to population growth. Only thirty-five to fifty percent of the eggs hatch: some are lost to predators, some from human disturbance, and some from other causes. Paradoxically, it was found that as the Red Rocks population grew, nesting success declined. Even after hatching, there is a further fifty percent loss of cygnets — why, nobody knows for sure. Mature birds die from many causes: in earlier times from hunting; today, predation from eagles and coyotes, lead poisoning from ingesting spent pellets with their food, starvation during the winter, and parasites — all take their toll. Nobody knows about their longevity either, although wild swans have been known to live in captivity for thirty-two years.

What was the size of this swan population before the 1931 census? Nobody knows. We do know, however, that since 1900 it had been tiny. From then on it grew, gradually but irregularly, from the sixty-nine in 1931 to 642 in 1954. In 1957, the population had declined to 488; a decline explained by the possibility of some birds temporarily having moved out of the area at census time. The present level of about seven hundred birds is what the habitat will tolerate, and for the last twenty years the population has remained relatively steady.

THE NORTHERN POPULATION

Meanwhile, what was happening to the British Columbia and Alaska populations? Although it was first established in 1869 that the trumpeter swan nested in Alaska, stories of migrating trumpeters were not believed, for they were thought to be whistlers. It is only in the last twenty years that their range and numbers have come to light. First of all, both in British Columbia and in Alaska, the populations are quite large — 2,848 birds were counted in 1968 and the actual number was probably over 3,400.

Many of these birds winter on open water in Alaska and in the interior of British Columbia. Others migrate south along the Pacific coast as far as the Columbia River. Despite complete protection, they are occasionally shot by irresponsible hunters who claim to mistake them for snow geese. In the autumn of 1976, just south of Vancouver, two were shot — by the same hunter.

THE SITUATION TODAY

Over the years, small groups of trumpeters have been relocated to other National Wildlife Refuges — Malheur in Oregon, Turnbull in Washington, La Creek in South Dakota, Elk in Wyoming, and Ruby Lake in Nevada. In these refuges, swans live free and breed successfully. Swans are also able to breed in captivity. The first time this happened was in 1870, in the London Zoo, and again at Slimbridge, in 1952. Today, the trumpeter swan, having survived its brush with extinction, appears quite safe — thanks to the men and funds of the United States Fish and Wildlife Service.

Aleutian Canada Goose

(Branta canadensis leucopareia)

As the icecap withdrew northward some eleven thousand years ago, new habitat became available to migratory birds. The range expanded and new groups formed. The range became vast; groups became isolated from others of their kind (at least during the breeding season); food and nesting conditions were different in new areas. With succeeding generations, new characteristics emerged. Today, biologists argue which are full species, which subspecies. Be that as it may, evolution has perhaps divided the Canada goose into more subspecies than any other North American bird. Although the pattern remains the same, each has increasingly different characteristics of size, color, and voice. The Canada now has a confusing array of subspecies, ranging from the tiny cackling Canada goose (*Branta canadensis minima*), weighing about three pounds, to the giant Canada goose (*Branta canadensis maxima*), weighing up to twenty-four. The Aleutian is a small goose, similar in pattern to other Canadas but darker and with a short neck.

HISTORY

For thousands of years the Aleutian Canada goose (*Branta canadensis leucopareia*) bred throughout the Aleutian Islands, the Komandorskie Islands of Russia, and along the Asiatic coast. It provided food for Aleuts, for explorers, and for sealers; particularly during the bird's summer moult when it was flightless for about a month.

THE DECLINE

By the turn of the century it had disappeared from much of its range. Early in the nineteenth century, the Russians introduced Arctic foxes into the Komandorskie Islands, and between 1910 and 1930 fur farmers imported more foxes into the Aleutians. The effects were devastating — where geese had been seen by the thousand, they disappeared entirely. By 1940 fur farming was abandoned, but the foxes remained. Only on Buldir, a 4,250-acre volcanic island, a small breeding population of geese hung on. Buldir, unsuited to fur farming, was remote, mountainous, and lacked a good harbor, and foxes were never introduced here.

As late as 1973, almost nothing was known of the small Buldir population, but it was guessed to number about three hundred birds. It was known the birds had at one time wintered in California and Japan; where they wintered now, nobody was certain.

WHAT IS BEING DONE?

After the end of the Second World War, the manager of the Aleutian Islands National Wildlife Refuge and his assistants took the first steps to save the Aleutian goose. They destroyed the foxes on Amchitka Island, and substantially reduced the fox population on some of the other islands. In 1962, the team found the remnant goose population on Buldir. Goslings from Buldir were taken and reared in captivity; then reintroduced to islands which had been cleared of foxes.

In 1971, seventy-five geese were released on Amchitka. The release failed — the birds were never seen again. Observers

Aleutian Canada goose ▶

saw them leave, but none returned. Capturing goslings, transporting them to the Patuxent Wildlife Research Center in Maryland, raising them, and then reintroducing them successfully into the wild, was not the answer. By 1973 the outlook was bleak — the breeding area was reduced to one small island in the western Aleutians; nothing was known of the wintering ground; the population was down to a remnant few hundred.

Then the United States Fish and Wildlife Service established a formal recovery team and introduced a four-part recovery program. In brief:

- Habitat on previously occupied islands is made suitable for reintroduction of geese.
- Captive birds are bred for release.
- Birds are acclimatized before release and monitored after release.
- The wild flock is studied and protected in both their winter and summer habitat.

Needless to say, a program of this scope involves considerable expense and cooperation from public and private agencies, but the results have been promising.

Biologists from the United States Fish and Wildlife Service chose the islands of Agattu (55,000 acres), Nizki (3,000 acres), Amchitka (70,000 acres), and Kanaga (90,000 acres), as suitable habitat for the soon-to-be-reintroduced geese. These four islands are far enough away from each other to be safe from a total wipe-out, in case of earthquake or tidal wave. The first challenge was to eliminate the fox population from 218,000 acres — a major undertaking by any standards. Their efforts so far have been hampered by a government order of 1972 prohibiting the use of chemical toxicants on federal lands. The earlier, almost successful elimination of foxes on Amchitka after World War II had been achieved by the use of poisons, albeit with some temporary adverse impact on the gull, raven, and eagle populations. Guns and traps are reasonably effective, but do not insure complete elimination — one pair of foxes left is one too many. Fox removal is vital for success.

The second phase of the plan, the captive production of geese, has been in full swing since the first goslings were captured in 1963. Between 1966 and 1975, some 325 birds have been bred in various locations (dispersion reduces the risk of epidemics). The objective is two hundred goslings a year.

In May, 1974, forty-one geese were released on Agattu Island. Much was learned from the release. Four pairs nested and two were successful; the rest simply hung about in a flock all summer. The next task was to encourage these two and three-year-old birds to migrate. Nine geese were captured on Buldir during their moult, and brought to Agattu. Their job was to lead the other geese away (at that time their wintering ground had not been established). On September 4, the flock flew east. The result? Two banded birds were shot in northern California during the winter, one other was seen, but none returned to Agattu in 1975. From this experiment, it became clear that captive breeding is only successful if released birds can establish themselves and breed in the wild. To this end, breeding facilities are being established on Amchitka Island.

The fourth part of the recovery plan involves the study and protection of wild geese. That Buldir Island is the only remaining nesting ground has been known since 1962; nothing was known of the flock's habits or population. Nothing, that is, until the summers of 1974, 1975, and 1976, when a group of biologists lived on the island from mid-May until early September. They observed nests, and they banded goslings and mature birds during the flightless period. The group was careful to avoid disturbance. For example, no nests were sought until incubation was under way, for they knew that the nest would be abandoned if disturbed earlier. When nests were found, vegetation within one meter and five meters of each nest was carefully studied to determine habitat preferences.

Because of the work on Buldir Island, we now know something of this wild group's life. The geese arrive on the island early in May. They lay during the third and fourth week in May. They make their nests in grass, some three-feet high, which makes finding them difficult — especially since some nests are built on forty-five degree slopes. In 1974, thirty nests were found; in 1975, forty-five. Probably only one-quarter of the total were found because suitable searching days are so few. (Suitable searching days are just before hatching, in late June.) Nests contain an average of six eggs; eighty percent hatch. Some young birds are lost to gulls and bald eagles, but predation is not a serious problem.

Two weeks after hatching, goslings and, by then, flightless adults are captured and banded. Long-handled nets, which sometimes catch several goslings at a time, are used. Family groups are kept together until all are banded and weighed. They are then released. Non-breeding birds, never in flocks but in small groups thought to be families, have been observed. They are tolerated in the nesting territory by the breeding birds, supporting the family theory.

The banding of the summer of 1974 made it possible to locate wintering birds in California, and to take steps to protect them from hunters. During the winter of 1974-75, nine of the banded wild birds were shot and reported, as were two of the released birds. Hunters thus aided in determining the winter feeding range. In March, 1974, what appeared to be the main flock of Aleutian Canada geese was found on the coast of northern California at Castle Rock near Crescent City. From this coastal rock the flock flew inland to feed. This flock varied from 285 when first seen, to a peak of 790 by mid-April — far in excess of the earlier estimate of three hundred. Following reports of shooting, and, becoming aware of the flock's large size, the California Department of Fish and Game closed several areas to the hunting of *all* Canada geese for the following season. Similarly, reports of shooting of banded Aleutians in the Sacramento Valley in November, 1975, caused the closing of the season there. More shooting in extreme southern California and in Arizona closed these areas also.

We now know that the small flock from Buldir Island winters in California. Much of the time it mixes with other Canada geese; protection of all Canadas in the areas where the Aleutians are found is essential. Although the Aleutians are smaller and darker than most other Canadas, these differences are not apparent when seen over a gun barrel.

During October and November of 1975, some two hundred Aleutian Canada geese again were seen at Castle Rock, indicating that they stop off here both on the flight south and the flight north. They then appear to spread through the central part of the state, returning to Castle Rock in March. By mid-April, 1976, the flock had grown to nine hundred.

THE FUTURE

It is too early to judge the impact of the recovery efforts made so far. It is clear, however, that this goose is in no immediate danger. Whether or not the population has increased since its wintering habits were identified is not clear. As observation and knowledge increase, so does the population. Success depends on, first, re-establishing breeding sites on once-inhabited islands. (G. Vernon Byrd, leader of the recovery team, feels that if fifty breeding pairs can be established on two other islands, the Aleutian Canada goose should be reclassified from an endangered to a threatened species; if three sites are established, it need no longer be classified as threatened.) Second, all foxes must be removed from breeding islands. Third, the flock must continue to be protected during the hunting season until its numbers are secure. This, of course, means closing large areas to shooting of all Canadas — an unpopular move with hunters.

Giant
Canada Goose

(Branta canadensis maxima)

The early explorers, settlers, and hunters of the central plains of North America are long gone, but they have left behind monumental tales of the Canada goose. A Jackson County, Minnesota record circa 1900 still stands: a twenty-four-pound bird was shot. In 1915, a twenty-one-pound bird was shot in Missouri; in 1906, a twenty-two-pound bird was shot in South Dakota. The largest number of big birds taken has been in North Dakota, but many others have been taken in the western provinces of Canada, and in Oregon, California, Utah, Colorado, Texas, Iowa, Wisconsin, and Illinois. Of course, these nineteenth and early twentieth century accounts of huge birds cannot be authenticated; recent evidence, however, indicates they are true.

Often, unusually large geese were seen feeding at the edges of flocks of smaller birds, usually in family groups or in small flocks. In flight, they seldom mixed with other geese. They flew lower than other geese, with a slow, shallow wingbeat, their long, swan-like necks outstretched.

Before scientists began to determine subspecies, all animals which looked alike were assumed to be the same. We now know that Canada geese are divided into about a dozen races or subspecies, each with a more-or-less independent breeding range. Each subspecies has adjusted to its environment, and each has developed a distinct size, color, and pattern (although the differences in pattern are subtle). No doubt there will be further sub-classifications of Canada geese as knowledge of them increases.

HISTORY

Dr. Harold C. Hanson, in his book, *The Giant Canada Goose*, compiled much of the early material, and it was he who outlined the work of two other men, R.P. Holland and W.B. Mershon. These two discussed and corresponded for seventeen years, starting in 1922, when Holland wrote, "I have been working on the theory that there is a distinct species of big goose for the last ten years, but have never got very far with it. I have a pile of data here in my office, but nothing conclusive enough to convince the ornithologists that such a bird exists."

The ornithologists in this case were in the United States Bureau of Biological Surveys in Washington; Dr. Alexander Wetmore was particularly renowned.

For years Holland and Mershon sought recognition of the subspecies. They were certain it was distinct, and even debated what it should be named — either the Mershon or Mershon-Holland.

In 1939, William Mershon died at eighty-four — too soon for recognition. In 1944, a note in *The Auk* recorded: "The northern plains goose seems even to have the geographic qualifications of a subspecies." In 1951, Jean Delacourt in his monumental study of wild fowl first described it formally as the giant Canada goose (*Branta canadensis maxima*), the largest of its species.

To understand the niche of *maxima* it is necessary to relate it to the other large races of Canadas. The Atlantic Canada goose (*Branta canadensis canadensis*) breeds in Nova Scotia, Newfoundland, Anticosti, and Labrador; north to the tree line and

westward in Quebec to the height of land which eventually slopes into Hudson Bay. It winters from Nova Scotia to North Carolina. The Hudson Bay Canada goose (*Branta canadensis interior*) is a dark race, breeding around Hudson Bay and James Bay, and wintering southward from South Dakota to the Gulf Coast, North Carolina, and Florida. The western Canada goose (*Branta canadensis moffitti*) is lighter colored. It breeds from British Columbia southward to northern California, Utah, and Nevada; east to Wyoming and Montana. While these races do overlap somewhat at the borders of their ranges, they differ enough to be distinct.

Not all *maxima* are exceptionally large. In samples taken of a number of birds from several areas, the average was ten to eleven pounds, the equivalent of very large specimens of other races. The wingspan of the largest *maxima* exceeds seventy inches; the largest authenticated record is eighty-eight. Very large western Canada geese have a wingspan of sixty-six inches. *Maxima* is lighter colored than other races and has a pale mantle across the shoulders at the base of the neck. Most also have a white patch across the forehead above the eyes and much white showing in the black neck. The chin strap in *maxima* is more pronounced than in other races, extending farther around the head; the bill is more massive and the neck is longer (this is the only race which can bend its neck back on itself). *Maxima* is usually silent in flight (unlike other races). The voice, when heard, is lower pitched.

In 1951, after Delacourt recognized it as a subspecies, he reported a former *maxima* breeding range from North and South Dakota and Minnesota south to a line from Kansas to Arkansas, but by this time the giant Canada goose was assumed to be extinct. Hanson's studies, published in 1965, have demonstrated that the *maxima* was not extinct, and that its breeding range had extended farther across the prairies between Alberta, Saskatchewan, Manitoba, possibly western Ontario, Idaho, and Montana.

Before settlement by man, North Dakota and adjacent areas of South Dakota were its natural breeding ground. By the 1920s, the *maxima* was extirpated from its natural home; by 1930 all wild birds were gone from the present breeding ranges in the United States. Why?

Generations of enormous shooting pressure and agricultural development of the breeding marshes virtually eliminated it. By 1900 it had disappeared from Nebraska and Kansas; by 1906 from South Dakota. In Minnesota, settlers ate even the eggs and raised young in captivity to eat in the winter.

A letter quoted by Dr. Hanson and written in 1922, records: "From 1885 to 1890, geese were fairly plentiful..., although I am inclined to the opinion that they were very largely local birds. In those days I thought very little of species or exact weights, and although I killed a great many very large geese, which I am sure weighed over twelve pounds, I can recollect weighing only one. That was killed about 1888.... We killed one goose that I put on the scales after I reached home and which weighed something over sixteen pounds. I cannot recollect that it differed in markings or color from the other geese.... Some years ago at Heron Lake, Minnesota... I saw a stuffed goose which people there told me weighed twenty-four pounds.... It was simply enormous... but goose shooting has as you know long been a thing of the past.... This, I think, is due more to drainage and settling up of the country than to extermination (shooting)." In other states the story was the same.

THE SITUATION TODAY

Paradoxically, the *maxima* owes its survival to the very people who ravaged it — the hunters. For many years hobbyists have kept captive stocks, mainly to use as live decoys. It is from these stocks that the present population in the United States is descended. Transplanted to wild fowl refuges in the United States and Canada, the offspring are free-flying, and have reinhabited many of their surviving marshes.

Not until 1960 was the largest single population of giant Canadas recognized as such. The geese were found in Alberta, at the edges of prairie lakes and sloughs, and along the South Saskatchewan River, where they nest. Now numbering between fifteen and twenty thousand, they were there even when the race was thought to be extinct, but were thought to be *moffitti*.

Elsewhere, introductions into suitable habitat have been successful. Flocks tend to remain in their new areas, and, despite some hunting pressure, are expanding. For example, the numbers of birds at Rochester, Minnesota, grew from two hundred and fifty in 1952 to six thousand in 1964. This flock expanded rapidly because of high breeding success in its natural range following reintroduction, combined with low mortality from shooting, but there is, undoubtedly, an upper limit to any population, determined primarily by crowding of nesting sites — assuming that there is not over-shooting.

Many of the newly established flocks in the United States do not migrate to any great extent; some not at all. During a hard winter, however, they may be forced to move south in search of food and open water. They tend to spread out from their refuges during the nesting season if suitable habitat is within reasonable distance, for often they require more breeding space than the refuge supplies.

Non-breeding birds (usually those which have not yet reached sexual maturity), from both the United States and Canadian prairies make unusually long migratory flights to the northern tundra in spring, far beyond their breeding grounds. Here they summer and moult. (Birds banded in Minnesota and Texas were recovered by trapping on the Thelon River in the Northwest Territories in the summer of 1964.) Geese nesting on the Canadian prairies migrate southward in winter, spreading out widely across the central and southern states.

THE FUTURE

Identification of the giant Canada goose as a subspecies is meaningless in itself. However, as a result of identification, the bird's range has been more clearly established; its migratory patterns are becoming better known; its original habitat has been identified; and the ecological requirements of the race are better understood.

With this knowledge, it has been possible to take the necessary remedial action to preserve the giant goose. Twenty-five years ago *maxima* was thought to be extinct at the moment of its identification as a race; today the population exceeds seventy-five thousand birds. Remember, however, that this growth has not been from almost zero, as the prairie population of giant Canadas was previously assumed to be the western Canada goose (*moffitti*).

Whatever its history, numbers have grown enormously and the bird appears to be secure. It will remain so provided enough habitat remains for nesting and wintering.

Mexican Duck

(*Anas diazi*)

The arid highlands of Central Mexico do not normally come to mind when considering ideal duck habitat. The climate is dry and hot. Only semi-reliable summer rains fill the few marshes and lakes and nourish growth along riverbanks. But here arose a race of duck which adapted itself to the erratic water supply; it adjusted its numbers, and it became a nomad on its range. After the rains came, it nested wherever suitable cover had grown and wherever there was enough food to support the young.

RANGE

The range of this nomadic bird, the Mexican duck (*Anas diazi*), extends from the state of Pueblo, south of Mexico City, throughout most of the central highlands northward into the United States. Before its decline, it bred for some 250 miles into New Mexico, along the Rio Grande, westward on the Gila River to southeastern Arizona, and east into Texas. The total north-south extent of this range was approximately thirteen-hundred miles, with a number of gaps — particularly in the southern part of the border state of Chihuahua and northern Durango, where there were almost no wet areas for the duck to feed and nest.

APPEARANCE

Both male and female Mexican ducks are superficially similar to the widespread female mallard (*Anas platyrhynchos*). Both are large, mottled brown pond ducks, somewhat darker and smaller than the mallard, but paler than the black duck (*Anas rubripes*). Like the mallard, the Mexican duck has a blue patch on the speculum of the wing, bordered by narrow black and white bars. Where the female mallard has white outer tail feathers, the Mexican duck's are all brown. The sexes look almost the same, except in the bill — the male's bill is olive green, the female's has a black stripe across the top, which shades to olive. The female mallard has a yellow bill. Differences in the color of bills vary greatly not only between individuals but also between pure Mexican ducks and those which have interbred with mallards, making identification difficult.

SUBSPECIES OR SPECIES?

John P. Hubbard, the project leader of the endangered species program for the State of New Mexico, Department of Game and Fish, has recently thrown much light on the origin of this duck. First, let us look into its background.

The Mexican duck was first described in 1874 as a subspecies of the mallard. Since then, its true status has been the cause of much controversy. Is it a subspecies or merely a strain of the mallard? Dr. Hubbard, who has studied all aspects of the bird's range and life cycle as well as existing museum specimens, concludes that, at about the time of the last glacial period, the mallard came to North America from Asia. Gradually, it spread through the west from Alaska, meeting the Mexican duck in northern New Mexico several thousand years ago. Here, interbreeding began. He concludes that ". . . . there are those who will regard the Mexican duck and the mallard as

Mexican duck ▶

separate species. At this point there is no correct answer, but it is clear that the Mexican duck interbreeds and backcrosses massively with the mallard and that introgression is widespread."

What Dr. Hubbard is saying is that few Mexican ducks in the United States and neighboring northern Mexico are of a pure strain. Mallards breed only as far south as northern Mexico; but there is still about a three-hundred-mile overlap. Here, they interbreed freely (except in a few small pockets where the habitat is more suitable to the Mexican duck; in these pockets, the Mexican duck remains relatively pure).

HISTORY

Spanish explorers settled around the Rio Grande as early as 1540. Even before 1540, Pueblo Indians farmed the Rio Grande valley. The Spaniards started draining marshes and digging canals. Gradually the nature of the land changed — to favor the mallard. If this trend continues, hybridization will continue until the Mexican duck as a pure strain disappears entirely from this northern, overlapping range.

In Mexico, the mallard is known only as a winter visitor. Here, the Mexican duck gradually becomes purer the farther south one goes; and through most of the Mexican one-thousand-mile range it is unaffected by the mallard.

At one time, it was thought that the Mexican duck in New Mexico and Texas was sufficiently isolated from the Mexican population to rank as a separate subspecies, and the northern group was known as the New Mexican duck (*Anas diazi novimexicani*); the southern as the Mexican duck (*Anas diazi diazi*). Today, the consensus of opinion is that both groups are, in fact, the same race, but the northern race has changed because of hybridization. (Incidentally, *diazi* comes from Augustin Diaz, who was the director of the Mexican Geographical and Exploring Commission in 1886.)

HABITAT

The Mexican duck lives along the banks of rivers, and in lakes, ponds, and potholes. During the dry season it feeds mostly in the uplands and in fields, returning to whatever water it can find to rest and to drink. We know little of the duck's nesting habits, because few nests have ever been found — they are well hidden in deep grass close to water, usually at the end of an arched runway under vegetation. Nesting, in most areas, is finished by early June, although young have been seen much later; time of nesting depends on the timing of the summer rains.

During the summer, the population is widely scattered; during the winter, most birds move out of the northern part of their range, moving southward, mainly to the state of Jalisco.

THE DECLINE

In Mexico, the Mexican duck's habitat is deteriorating at an alarming rate. Overgrazing (by cattle) has eliminated the cover around potholes, causing them to dry up. Many of the larger marshy areas have been drained for farming. Standing water in lakes has been diverted, leaving them shrunken and alkaline. In areas where water remains, people or livestock have generally taken over. Today, the only suitable habitat left is along the marshy banks of rivers and canals. There is much variation in the suitability of the habitat from season to season, not only for nesting but also for winter congregation. That is, water sources have a tendency to dry out. In 1965, for example, in one mountain lake in Chihuahua, a thousand birds were seen; by the following year the lake had nearly dried up — and only one pair could be found. By 1967 the lake was full again and suitable for winter feeding.

THE SITUATION TODAY

Since 1947, the United States Fish and Wildlife Service has been monitoring the Mexican duck population in both the United States and Mexico, mostly by aerial survey. According to their counts, numbers have fluctuated enormously, from 780 birds in 1951 to 14,760 in 1970. The Mexican duck is, however,

quite migratory; also, it changes its habitat according to the habitat's suitability. These factors probably account for the wild fluctuations in numbers. The censuses did not always cover the same areas and the ducks may have moved on to another area while the censuses were being taken. Population fluctuations are caused by the vagaries of the weather — the higher the level of water in nesting areas, the more birds.

By 1960 the duck population in the United States had shrunk to one hundred and fifty. At that time the New Mexico Department of Fish and Game started a recovery program. It began to rear ducks in captivity for release to the wild. So far, several hundred birds have been released (although the program at present is slowing down). The results? By 1975, because of this program, the Mexican duck population in Arizona was reckoned to be ninety-five; in New Mexico, two to three hundred; in Texas, a hundred to a hundred and fifty. The total population today is somewhere between 450 and 650. In Mexico, the population, is of course, much larger. In 1975, an aerial survey counted fourteen thousand birds in Jalisco and adjacent states; the total population today is about forty thousand. (This number, according to Dr. Hubbard, is all the remaining habitat can stand.)

While Mexican numbers are encouraging and the United States population is on the rise, it is likely that the bird's habitat, because of encroaching agricultural expansion, will continue to shrink, and the Mexican duck's future remains in doubt — even in Mexico.

California Condor

(Gymnogyps californianus)

The condor is a giant bird — nine feet from wing tip to wing tip. It is by far the largest land bird in North America. Adults are black, except for the white lining on the underside of the wing. There is a black collar or ruff around the neck. The neck and head are bare, and, as with other vultures, the skin here is red or orange. The hooked bill and legs are gray.

It is a thing of no great beauty, except in the air — where it soars with an effortless freedom constantly searching for food.

Today, there are only about fifty condors left.

THE BEGINNING

While the condor population has probably never been large, the present remnant represents only a small fraction of what it was before California was settled by white men. Since the eighteenth century the bird's range has been reduced to its present breeding and feeding range in the coastal mountains of southern California; originally, the condor extended from British Columbia in the north to Baja California in the south. It is thought that, as late as the nineteenth century, a permanent population, separate from the California group, lived around the Columbia River in Oregon. No nests were ever found; probably because nobody ever looked for them. Records from the nineteenth century are sparse. We do know that birds from the northern areas were eliminated by about 1850, mainly through shooting and human interference of their habitat.

THE SITUATION TODAY

Today, all remaining condors live in a range of horseshoe-shaped mountains in California. The western prong is to the northwest of Los Angeles along the coast, the northeastern on the western slope of the Sierra Nevadas. The nesting range is in the southern portion — in three distinct areas of San Luis Obispo, Santa Barbara, and Ventura Counties. Here live all the world's surviving California condors. Their continued existence depends largely on the efforts of the United States Fish and Wildlife Service (presently represented by a dedicated biologist, Sanford R. Wilbur); the California Department of Fish and Game; and the National Audubon Society. Without their help, the condor would probably be extinct.

What have these agencies done, and what more can they do to save the giant, soaring vultures from extinction? To find the answer, we must consider the bird and its relationship to its environment.

LIFE CYCLE

The life cycle of the condor is not conducive to population explosion. Each female lays only one egg per clutch and that usually only every second year. If the first egg is destroyed, however, it has been known to lay a second. Incubation lasts about fifty days, and, when hatched, the young bird remains in its cave or crevice for a further five months. It is unable to fly until about seven months old. It remains dependent on its parents for a further three-month period, thus keeping the parents bound to the vicinity of the nest site for about a year.

California condor ▶

Juveniles reach sexual maturity at about six years, and are then capable of reproduction for twenty years or more. (Some individuals even live to forty.) In theory, it would seem that each pair is capable of producing twenty or more young during its lifetime. For reasons which are not clear, the research of the last few decades does not support this theory. Even with complete protection, reasonably adequate food supplies, and minimum disturbance in the nesting areas, only about twelve young were hatched between 1968 and 1975 — a net reduction in the population of perhaps five. It seems that at least two young are required per year to maintain the already tiny population, in which, ominously, the average age is gradually increasing.

During the winter, most condors congregate in the area of the Sespe Condor Sanctuary, although a few birds remain to the northwest in the coast range. An observation post has been established in this area at the head of an access corridor within the sanctuary, some fifteen miles north of Fillmore, California. Here, one may reasonably expect to see condors leaving their roosting areas in the morning and returning at night. Sometimes they are sighted even during the day. In late spring and summer, most of the non-breeding birds wander both northwest and northeast along fairly narrow corridors along the coastal range and the Sierra Nevada mountains. Another observation site, suitable from July to September, has been established at Mount Pinos, some thirty miles north of the Sespe Condor Sanctuary. Information about how to reach these sites is available from the National Audubon Society, 1973 South Victoria Avenue, Ventura, California 93003. The telephone number is (805) 644-3789.

THE DECLINE

Condors require about two pounds of meat a day. They feed only on the carcasses of dead animals, preferring reasonably fresh meat, although they will take meat in varying stages of decay. Before white settlement of the west, elk, pronghorn antelope, mule deer, and ground squirrels were common in the area. Deer were never a major source of food, for they tended to die in canyons and brush, and their carcasses were usually inaccessible.

Let us look at the situation today. Squirrels are much scarcer because of poison control programs; the sick animals retreat to their burrows to die. Settlement has introduced cattle, sheep and horses, which do replace wild food adequately for most of the year, but not during the summer when mortality is low. Improved ranching conditions, better herd control, and the early removal of carcasses have further reduced the condor's food supply. Since 1900, sheep flocks have been dwindling and cattle have not replaced them as a reliable food source.

Food within reasonable foraging distance of the nesting areas is vital to breeding success. Weak birds tend not to nest, and, when they do, now require long flights to feed themselves and their young. Long periods away from the nest lead to poor hatching ratios because eggs get cold; and also result in weak or starved chicks. Here lies the principal problem. Non-breeding birds are not affected, for they are not bound to the nesting site, and, for them, food supplies are normally adequate.

Urban growth has directly reduced the area available for feeding by about fifteen per cent, but, indirectly, by much more. As has been mentioned already, a trend to smaller ranches means that carcasses are quickly discovered and as quickly removed. Although there is no evidence to suggest that condors are starving, the reduction of food in the nesting areas has reduced the condor's capacity to breed.

WHAT IS BEING DONE?

The support of private land owners has been enlisted. They are encouraged not to remove the carcasses of dead animals and to leave them undisturbed.

Equally important, a supplemental feeding program was initiated in 1971. Carcasses, usually mule deer which have been killed on the roads, are placed in a suitable feeding area. (This involves the storage of frozen bodies and their transportation to the site on light, hand-hauled carts.) In the initial two-year study period, eighty-three carcasses were offered with considerable success. Nine were removed by bears before condors could feed, but feeding was observed on forty-seven and assumed from evidence on twenty-seven others. While no assumptions of this feeding program's impact on breeding success can yet be made, three young were raised in the Sespe Condor Sanctuary between 1971 and 1973, compared with only one in 1970.

Human interference caused the condor's downfall — perhaps it will also help it to survive. As part of a 1973 study of past distribution of the California condor, Sanford Wilbur, the leader of the recovery team, found one hundred and eighty-five specimens, fifty-one skeletons, and fifty-five eggs in museums — the evidence of two hundred and ninety-one birds, or, five times the existing population. To this number must be added the unknown number which died naturally, and the many shot, poisoned, and caught in traps.

Today, people are aware of the condor's plight, but interference caused by human curiosity and noise are the new hazards.

During the nesting period, adult birds are easily disturbed, particularly early or late in the day. The presence of man within five hundred yards of the nest may cause both parents to abandon it for several hours, often long enough to cause death or egg chilling. The parents invariably return, but by then it may be too late to save the egg. Loud noises, such as sonic booms and blasting, make the sitting bird leap from its nest (really not a nest, for the egg is laid on the ground in a crevice or shallow cave). The noise of a truck more than a mile away may cause a bird to flush — posing the danger of breaking the egg or harming the chick. Curiously, flying birds are undisturbed by man. They show great interest, especially in response to arm waving and shouting, and will fly quite close.

It cannot be repeated often enough: freedom from disturbance within the condor's nesting and roosting area is essential to its survival. Three-quarters of the known nesting sites are in a 200,000-acre area, some sixty road miles northwest of Los Angeles, of which the Sespe Condor Sanctuary constitutes 53,000 acres. Most of this range is mountainous and relatively inaccessible, but even here conservationists wage a constant struggle against development — housing, oil drilling, water impoundment, and recreation. Freedom from disturbance from roads, boats, and hikers near nesting sites is vital. Although the sanctuary provides full protection, the surrounding area must also remain unchanged. Traditional roosting sites, either stands of trees or cliffs, are used year after year. Changes in these sites make them unattractive to condors and affect their breeding potential. Even now some roosting sites are dangerously close to cottages and oil rigs; fortunately, most are about a mile from the nearest source of disturbance.

THE FUTURE

The condor has been doomed to extinction for a hundred years, but still it clings to life. The greatest problem facing it is its incapacity to increase from the present two or so birds a year. Adequate food near the nesting area is essential, as is the absence of disturbance. Both are controllable given financial resources and the goodwill of the public.

What are the condor's chances? Sanford R. Wilbur, who probably knows better than anyone else, wrote in the February, 1976 edition of *The Environmental Journal*:

> At this point, we don't know. The species is certainly more endangered than ever before; thus the situation is extremely critical. On the other hand, the desire to save the condor is great and the current level of cooperation among state, federal, and private organizations is high, perhaps as high as for conservation of any other species of wildlife. If the population still has the capability of sustaining itself, then we can be at least cautiously optimistic that the shadows of soaring condors will still flow over California's ridges and canyons for yet a few more years.

Southern Bald Eagle

(Haliaeetus leucocephalus leucocephalus)

Graceful and agile it certainly is, but the bald eagle, sup-
posedly symbolic of power, courage, steadfastness, and grace
is a robber of the catch of other species. It is timid and
cowardly and feeds largely on carrion. The golden eagle
(*Aquila chrysaetos canadensis*), known as the king of birds,
better represents the noble characteristics expected of a national emblem.

On the credit side, the bald eagle does exude a mesmerizing
power as it flies — the wings beat slowly, the air whistles
through stiff feathers. Soaring, it wheels as it rides the ther-
mals to great heights.

When chosen as the United States emblem in 1782, the bald
eagle was typically North American. It bred from Alaska to
Ungava, from Florida to California. Except for a population in
northern Siberia, America was its home; let us hope America
will remain its home.

THE DECLINE

Bald eagles are easily disturbed at the nest and are prone to
desert when disturbed. Encroaching civilization and cottages
put pressure on their breeding areas long before DDT did its
devastating work. In common with other fish eaters, egg

thinning began about 1950, reducing nesting success in the worst affected areas to one young to each four nesting pairs. As with other contaminants, DDT residues build up in the eagle's tissues in ever-increasing amounts — they reduce the calcium content of the egg shells, and the eggs break. DDT is also present in the eggs themselves and renders many birds infertile. The use of DDT was banned in 1972, and it is hoped that nesting success will improve. So far, it is too early to draw any conclusions.

NESTS

Bald eagles are essentially sedentary by nature, except for birds in Alaska and other northern areas, where they must move to open water in winter to find fish and other prey. In southern areas they prefer to remain in the vicinity of their nests for most of the year. The eagle's nest is indeed its castle. It is the home to which adult birds return to roost and feed long after they have driven off their fledged young; the same nest is used for many years. Most are at or near the top of tall trees — preferably pines. Nests are built of sticks, some several feet long and up to half an inch in diameter. Objects as large as corn stalks may even be used. Nesting material is mostly provided by the male, while the female appears to do all the building.

In the first year the structure may be only two feet deep and four or five feet wide, but is firmly placed in a position where it is supported by branches. In later years, more material is added to the top and sides of the nest until, after twenty years, it may be fifteen feet deep and eight feet wide. At the center is a cup two feet across and a few inches deep which is lined with finer material — twigs, grass, hair, and feathers. In time it becomes flattened with use and compacted as the materials wear down. As the nest grows, the lower strata rot away, requiring constant renewal.

Nests have been known to remain in use for as long as thirty-five years. Eventually they become so heavy they weaken the tree. Records do exist of nests built on the ground, even in low places, and, in the north, cliffs and high ledges are often used. Here, the nest may be little more than a few twigs.

LIFE CYCLE

Bald eagles mature when about five years old, and it is only then that they achieve the pure white head and tail and blackish plumage for which they are so well known. Before maturity, bald eagles progress through varying shades of dark brown, when they are almost indistinguishable from golden eagles. Eagles mate for life. Two eggs are usually laid, but sometimes one or three. Incubation lasts about thirty-five days, with the two young hatching four days apart. The second hatchling, being smaller, is frequently neglected by the parents and victimized by the older bird. It may starve.

The young remain in the nest for about ten weeks. In the tenth week they are capable of some flight, often perching on the edge of the nest, leaping several feet in the air, and soaring directly above the nest. In order to get the young to leave the nest, parents discontinue feeding and lure the young away with fish or other prey.

Fish is the eagle's main diet. When available, dead or dying fish of up to four or five pounds are picked up from the water's surface or at water's edge. At the nest, the catch is torn apart and small pieces are fed to the young. In the south, catfish and bass are most commonly caught; in the northwest, spawning salmon are eaten in summer. Here, eagles feed with bears and ravens.

Eagles also often associate with ospreys and rob them regularly. The osprey, returning to its nest with a fish clutched in its talons, is attacked, and usually forced to drop its prey. The eagle then seizes the osprey's prey in mid-air. Eagles have been known to swoop below the osprey, and, twisting in the air, seize the fish from the osprey's claws.

When necessary, eagles are quite capable of catching healthy fish themselves. They then plunge into the water in the manner of the osprey, and may submerge completely before capturing their fish.

Ducks, geese, coots, shorebirds, squirrels, and rabbits are all taken for food. Eagles reach remarkable bursts of speed when chasing ducks and can even overtake them. They harass ducks from the air, forcing them to dive until they are exhausted. When the hapless duck takes to the air, it is almost certainly doomed. Geese present a problem when killed on the water, for they may be too heavy for the eagle to carry away. It then flaps along, dragging the goose to shore.

THE SITUATION TODAY

Bald eagles are recognized in two races — the southern (*Haliaeetus leucocephalus leucocephalus*) and the northern (*Haliaeetus leucocephalus alascanus*). The differences are too subtle to be observed, but the farther north, the larger the bird. Florida birds have an average wing length of twenty-one inches, those in New England twenty-three inches, and those in Alaska twenty-four inches. The line of demarcation is open to debate. A.C. Bent, in his monumental *Life Histories*, suggests, "the line should be drawn somewhat south of North Carolina and.... .. restricted to birds of the Lower Austral Zone."

Under the terms of the Endangered Species Preservation Act of 1966, the 40th Parallel was arbitrarily used to separate the two races. In a symposium a few years ago, Roger Tory Peterson, the well-known ornithologist and artist, said, "all those that are not in Alaska or in the northwest coast of Canada" are the southern race. Wherever the dividing line, the bald eagle population in the north is prospering. Alaska alone has some seventy-five hundred breeding pairs, indicating a total population of perhaps twenty-five thousand. The coast of British Columbia has a large but uncounted population — this despite a bounty system which was in effect for many years, starting in 1917. It is tragic to think that the number killed may have exceeded 100,000.

It is the southern bald eagle that is on the endangered species list. A survey of the United States population taken in 1974 indicates that the number of breeding pairs in the lake states of Minnesota, Wisconsin, and Michigan was 318; in Florida, 150; in the northwest, 101; in the Chesapeake Bay area, 56; in Maine, 33; and in all other areas, 50 — a total of only 708 pairs! Some 551 young were produced that year, showing an overall success rate of .78 young per nest. The success rate of the Maine population was the worst, at .38. It had, however, improved from the previous year's low of .23 young per nest, presumably due to the lessening impact of DDT.

A somewhat petulant note in *The Auk*, quarterly publication of the American Ornithologists' Union, of October, 1975 stated that popular articles, including some by ornithologists, continue to depict the southern bald eagle as an endangered species, thereby calling public attention to it when many other species are in much greater need. *The Auk* concludes that the bald eagle is in trouble in Maine and may have declined overall during the past twenty-five years, but that the bird occurs continent-wide in much larger numbers than many would have us believe.

At present there are no recovery programs; it is hoped that with the lessening of DDT's impact, the population will increase naturally.

Florida Everglade Kite

(Rostnamus sociabilis plumbeus)

The kite grasps the apple snail in its talon and flies to a low perch. Here, on a bush or in an abandoned nest, it waits, motionless. A few minutes later the snail begins to open, the kite grasps the snail with the point of its beak, detaches it from the shell, and swallows it. The shell, intact, is discarded. The kite's continued existence depends on the snail. Until 1971, the apple snail (*Pomacea paludosa*), was thought to be the Everglade kite's only food. That year, Paul W. Sykes, Jr., a biologist with the United States Fish and Wildlife Service and principal authority on the Florida Everglade kite, saw something extraordinary: a kite eating a turtle. In 1972, his associate, Herbert W. Kale II, saw a kite feeding on a small mammal — probably a rice or cotton rat.

Despite these two aberrations, the Everglade kite is one of the world's most highly specialized birds — both in its feeding and habitat requirements. It is also the second rarest bird in the United States (after the California condor), and there is a correlation between its rarity and its specialization. Extreme specialization of habitat and food add to any animal's problems of survival; relying on only one source of food can lead to a speedy end if the food disappears. This is what is happening to the Florida Everglade kite.

APPEARANCE

It is quite a large bird, some fifteen inches long with a forty-four-inch wingspan. The male has a slate gray body, longish black head, dark wings, red legs, and red feet. The tip of the tail is white, as is the wide band at the base of the tail, making it unmistakable in the field. The beak is sharp and hooks down at the tip. The female is larger than the male, brown streaked where the male is dark gray. The legs and face are orange, where the male's are red.

HISTORY AND HABITAT

The Everglade, or snail kite, is one of four kite species in the United States. All are hawk-like birds; all are in trouble. The Everglade kite is a northern subspecies of the widespread snail kites. Of the subspecies it is the only one in danger — one race in Cuba, one in Central America, and one from Panama to Argentina — are holding their own. So much so that a few years ago Roger Tory Peterson described seeing about two hundred kites in "one milling flock" in the Amazon.

In 1974, a careful count was made of the Florida subspecies. Only eighty-one birds were found, while in 1964, the United States Fish and Wildlife Service had estimated a population of no more than fifteen — an increase of sixty-six. What happened? And why?

At the turn of the century, the Everglade kite bred throughout the Everglades, south almost to Cape Sable, and east to Miami. Then the Everglades was filled with water for most of the year; only some sections dried out in the dry season. The Everglades, a remarkable "river," flows gently for some hundred miles south from Lake Okeechobee. It is about thirty miles wide and only a few feet deep even in the wet season. Lake Okeechobee is also a mixture of open water and marshes, but with clearly defined borders. Some forty miles long and

Florida Everglade kite ▶

thirty miles wide, it is near the center of the Florida peninsula, one third of the way up from the southern tip. The lake's drainage nourishes the Everglades with fresh water, creating sawgrass marshes, cypress swamps, wet prairies, and some open water. Areas a foot or two above the level of the water (hammocks) support an exotic growth of palms, trees, and plants.

Early in the century a huge undertaking was begun — draining parts of the Everglades, primarily to create land suitable for agriculture. It has taken a terrible toll on the Everglade kite population. By 1930, A.C. Bent, the great compiler of the *Life Histories*, could find only one in the Everglades. Vast areas south of Okeechobee had dried out, the apple snail had nearly disappeared, and, with it, the kite. But a fair number of birds still nested along the length of the St. Johns River, which flows southwest parallel to the east coast of Florida. Today, the population in this area is restricted to a few water impoundments at the headwaters of the river. South of the Okeechobee a few kites still exist in the northern edge of the Everglades National Park and in a strip to the north where there is still enough water to produce a supply of snails.

Demand for fresh water in Florida is prodigious. The original Everglades drainage opened new land for farming and citrus growing, but lowering the water level created a demand for water for irrigation for the land which had been cleared. The geriatric boom has ebbed and flowed with the fortunes of the economy, but the domestic demands for water from a growing population have always been at the expense of the Everglades and the St. Johns River Basin.

Other species have been adversely affected. The Cape Sable sparrow's range has been altered, and limpkins, herons, galinules, ibises, and bitterns are also much restricted.

Lack of water (and snails) is not the only reason for the kite's decline. The water hyacinth is another. A floating plant with tiny leaves, it can completely cover the water's surface, and make it almost impossible for the kite to find snails under water. The large apple snails spend much of the day below the surface, emerging only in the morning and late afternoon, clinging to sawgrass and cattails. The kite hovers on wide, rounded wings, taking snails either below the surface by thrusting its talons into the water, or, above the surface, when snails emerge into the marsh vegetation. If it cannot find snails under water, its hunting is seriously curtailed.

As has been said earlier, the kite's specialized habitat requirements also work against it. In its marsh, it needs the proper combination of open water, cattails, sawgrass, or other large emergent grasses; as well as bushes or small trees for perching and nesting. These conditions have to exist in an area with a low and distant horizon for visibility, and with enough permanent water to keep the area from going dry. The male builds the nest of sticks and grasses, in cattails or in a shrub or tree, no more than eight feet or so above the water. The nest's loose construction and its location in fragile grasses makes it vulnerable to destruction by enemies or to tipping in high winds.

Shooting also, particularly during the duck season, has put pressure on the Everglade kite, despite legal protection and much publicity. Kites do have one defense — their nomadic nature. They nest in loose colonies, but after the young are fledged, they wander widely and establish new colonies in suitable areas.

THE SITUATION TODAY

Most remaining birds nest in the marshes in the southwest corner of Lake Okeechobee. In this area almost all nests are built in cattails. But often cattails are not strong enough to stand the nest's and parent bird's weight. Other nests are lost because of winds, predation from mammals, snakes, and ants.

In 1973, in an effort to improve nesting success, Paul Sykes introduced an artificial nesting platform — an open, basket-like structure made of woven galvanized strips of metal placed on a galvanized pipe. Only nests in particularly exposed locations and in fragile cattails were disturbed. When laying

began, nests were moved one at a time. The basket was mounted at the precise height of the nest and in the same spot; the whole nest was then placed in the basket. The results were encouraging. Parent birds accepted the platform, and two of the four nests moved produced a total of five young. The others were lost to predators.

What must be done to save the Everglade kite? As Paul Sykes says:

> In view of the continuing destruction of wetlands, it is imperative that suitable areas within the historic range be purchased and managed for the Everglade kite if this raptor is to remain a part of the fauna of Florida and the United States. Areas in and around the Loxahatchee National Wildlife Refuge should be developed and managed to their fullest potential for the species. Better protection is also needed during the hunting season. Nesting areas with at least a one-fourth mile buffer zone should be closed to entry and rigorously protected. Adequate surface waters should be maintained on a permanent basis in these areas used frequently by kites. Research into all aspects of its biology should be continued. In particular, high priority should be given to a study of the life history and ecological requirements of its exclusive food source, the apple snail.

It is obvious that recovery will be difficult and expensive, and to quote Paul W. Sykes again, "The present status of the Florida subspecies is . . . highly critical and there is a very real danger that it may become extinct in the near future if present trends continue."

American Peregrine Falcon

(Falco peregrinus anatum)

Peregrines are spectacular birds to watch.

Cream-colored below, dark bluish-gray above, they have white faces with dark mustaches. The female, or tiercel, is the larger — it is about twenty-one inches long, has a wingspan of over forty inches, yet weighs only two pounds. The wings are long and pointed, with a decided backward bend at the elbow.

The flight is regular; the wingbeats are rapid and deep on both up and down strokes. When hunting, the peregrine rises to considerable heights, and, on seeing its flying prey, goes into a steep, powered dive, known as the stoop. Estimates of its speed in the stoop range to 275 miles an hour. Its speed has been officially measured at 180 — among the fastest of all animals.

There are three recognized subspecies of peregrines in North America:

- American peregrine falcon (*Falco peregrinus anatum*)
- tundra peregrine (*Falco peregrinus tundrius*)
- Peal's peregrine (*Falco peregrinus pealei*)

Whatever one may feel about the fussiness of subspecific differences in races of the same species, it will make our story more interesting if we understand the habits and ranges of the three recognized peregrine races.

The *anatum* race still breeds in tiny numbers in the western United States. Formerly, it bred from Mexico to the northern forests of Canada and Alaska. In its prime, this somewhat sedentary group moved southward only moderately in winter — only far enough to be comfortable. The second subspecies, the *tundrius*, is smaller and paler. It nests in the arctic islands, the tundra regions of Alaska and Canada, and Greenland. The *tundrius* group is migratory, over-flying North America to winter mostly in South America. The third group, the *pealei*, does not move far in winter from its breeding grounds in the Aleutians and Queen Charlotte Islands. It stays in remote, unsettled areas all-year round, and is, consequently, far less exposed to DDT. (DDT has been the principal cause of the peregrine's decline.)

THE SITUATION TODAY

The American peregrine and the tundra peregrine have been recognized as endangered species by the United States Fish and Wildlife Service since 1968. By then, they had disappeared as breeding birds east of the Rocky Mountains. In the Alaskan and Canadian arctic and in Greenland, nesting continued, but the population was declining. In the western United States, the situation was critical — where five hundred eyries had flourished, by 1975 there were fewer than one hundred breeding pairs left. The northwestern Peal's peregrine, which breeds in the Queen Charlotte Islands and in the Aleutians, remains stable. The subject of our story is the American peregrine falcon, and, to a lesser extent, the tundra peregrine.

NESTING AND FEEDING HABITS

Before 1950, a healthy, though small population nested in the eastern United States and in Canada — in the Hudson Palisades, in gorges, on sea cliffs, and even on ledges of bridges and high buildings.

One famous pair nested on a ledge of the St. Regis Hotel in New York. The most exciting nest of all (to me at least, for I used to see it regularly) was on the roof of the Sun Life Building in Montreal. Between 1938 and 1952, the pair returned regularly every summer and several times successfully raised their young in the very middle of the huge city. They fed well on the city's supply of pigeons and house sparrows, and were frequently seen making kills in the park to the west of the Sun Life Building.

Most peregrines, however, nest on high points near the seacoast, where they prey mainly on shore birds, ducks, and gulls. Inland, they will take grouse and pheasants, but prefer smaller birds such as swallows, jays, and blackbirds. With its enormous speed, the peregrine can overtake any other bird — and does. It strikes quickly, with great force; the talons first cause an explosion of loose feathers, then kill instantly. It may immediately take the victim in its talons and fly to a suitable place to feed, or, it may first let the dead bird fall to the ground.

Observers have seen peregrines harrying flocks of shorebirds and pigeons for an hour or more at a time. They stoop, and, in a rush, intentionally pass the frightened birds. They then climb and do it again and again. Perhaps they do it for practice, perhaps even for fun. The presence of a falcon sends wading birds into a nervous frenzy, and no wonder.

THE DECLINE

What caused the crash of the falcon population, not only in North America, but over most of the world? As we said earlier, DDT was the principal cause. DDT was first used extensively for agricultural spraying in 1946. Knowing what we know now of the dangers of this poison, it is frightening to remember with what abandon it was first used. For example, photographs taken after World War II show groups of refugees lined up for delousing: their faces and bodies white from DDT

American peregrine falcon ▶

powder. They were deloused — and perhaps irrevocably poisoned. Unfortunately, it still goes on, only the formulae are different. New drugs are sold before their impact is understood. Thalidomide fifteen years ago, and, more recently, the swine flu vaccine, are cases in point.

In the case of the falcon and other birds of prey, DDT's impact was indirect. Not many died from feeding on DDT-tainted prey. The consequences were more insidious — the birds became unable to reproduce.

When sprayed on the soil, DDT remains toxic for many years. It is ingested by insects, who die. The surviving insects, in turn, are eaten by small birds and other animals, and so up the food chain — each feeder carrying increased concentrations of DDE (a form of DDT residues). The end of the chain is the large bird of prey. Here the poison stays, affecting the hormones and weakening reproductive cycles. The first symptom is a thin egg shell. Fewer and fewer young hatch, because the weight of the parent breaks the eggs.

The peregrine continued to lay eggs, but some were infertile, or they failed for other reasons. Finally, the Sun Life birds were seen eating their own eggs; other eggs disappeared one by one, year after year.

Falcons are long-lived birds, but they suffer heavy casualties before reaching sexual maturity — a sixty-percent mortality rate is estimated. Their reproductive process is slow, despite the three to five eggs laid, for they do not breed until three or four years of age.

A striking example of their vulnerability occurred in England. During World War II, homing pigeons were still extensively used as a means of communication — mostly by resistance groups in occupied Europe. In England, peregrines were taking these pigeons, and a determined campaign was begun to reduce the peregrine. Young and eggs were destroyed; flying birds were shot on sight. The campaign was so successful that by 1945 few were left. Surprisingly, the population had recovered substantially by 1950. Thereafter the decline was precipitous — it takes about three years for DDT to make its impact.

Nor are arctic birds immune. During the summer, they feed on migrants who have brought the poison with them; on migration and in South America (where DDT is still extensively used), they are again exposed.

In 1971, the use of DDT was banned in Canada; in 1972, in the United States. The road back, if there even is one, will be long — particularly for loons and hawks. Toxicity remains in the soil for ten years or more, and in the tissues of birds and other animals for much longer.

Although a slight improvement has already been noted in contamination levels in the eggs of other hawks, it is too late for the *anatum* race. In the east, it cannot re-establish naturally: there, the American falcons are probably all gone. There is hope that a few pairs have survived in the northern forests, but it is a remote one, and there is certainly no reason to suppose that the tundra race (on which release experiments are being conducted) would, on its own, repopulate the east.

WHAT IS BEING DONE?

In both the United States and Canada, conservationists are trying to reintroduce the peregrine into its southern range. Several programs are in hand, involving raising birds in captivity for release, as well as building captive stocks with which to work. We shall comment only on two of the programs: one, sponsored by the Canadian Wildlife Service, centered in Wainwright, Alberta, and another, sponsored by a number of public and private agencies at Cornell University in Ithaca, New York. The agencies include the university, the United States Army Matériel Command, the United States Fish and Wildlife Service, the National Audubon Society, the United States Forest Service, and the World Wildlife Fund. Early results of both programs are encouraging — captive breeding is going well. It will, however, be some time yet before the programs can claim total success. The big test is whether released birds will return to nest.

THE CANADIAN EXPERIMENTS

What are the programs? In Canada, twelve immature tundra peregrines were captured which, together with a few gyrfalcons (*Falco rusticolus*) and prairie falcons (*Falco mexicanus*), formed the nucleus of a continuing experiment which began in 1970. There were many problems of pairing, diet, breeding, and incubation to overcome, but all species bred successfully. With a base of several pairs breeding in captivity, efforts were begun to introduce them to the wild. Eggs of captive peregrines were placed under the more numerous wild prairie falcons for hatching and fledging. Again, this was successful. It did not, however, answer the question of imprinting — will the young imprint so much on their foster parents that they will be unable to breed? (Imprinting is learning, occurring rapidly and very early in life.)

In 1974 and 1975, eggs were placed under wild peregrines in the arctic who hatched and raised the young as their own. To induce wild peregrines to raise more young than they would normally, the first clutch of eggs was taken from the nest, artificially hatched, and the young were raised (temporarily) in captivity. The female, meanwhile, relaid. The first set of young was then placed in one of the nests, the second brood in the second nest built when the first eggs were taken. The parents raised both broods. This technique, of course, does not reintroduce peregrines to areas where they once bred, but it does enlarge the wild population.

Another experiment, using the downy young of prairie falcons, was tried in anticipation of later using peregrines for the same experiment. Some twenty-three young were placed in the nests of three other hawk species, outside the usual range of the prairie falcon. All were accepted, and only two died before fledging. (Later, one was killed by an automobile hundreds of miles from the nesting site, proving that this bird, at least, had been able to hunt for itself.)

THE CORNELL EXPERIMENTS

For at least three thousand years falcons have been trained for hunting — in Europe and Asia as a sport for the nobility; in parts of the East as a method of obtaining food. Larger raptors (birds of prey) are still used today to kill foxes, hares, wild goats, even animals as large as wolves.

The Cornell experiments (conducted by Dr. T.J. Cade) are based on the belief that by reversing the training process, falcons can be induced to revert to the wild. In this they have been successful, but, whether or not falcons will return to nest in the area of their release is still unknown. Dr. Cade and others involved in the experiment have long been falconers. As such, they understand the nature of the birds. Their experience and their devotion to the species has made the Cornell group ideally suited to the project.

The technique which falconers use to train young captive birds is called hacking. This consists of feeding an immature bird at the same place, "the hack board," every day. (The hack board may be a stump or a board.) When fledged, the immature falcon is allowed to fly free until it learns to kill for itself. Then it must be brought under control quickly, for it would soon lose the instinct to return to the hack board.

At Cornell, the young are hatched from incubated eggs. When they are one week old, they are placed in cages with adult peregrines — thus hopefully imprinting on their own kind rather than on humans. When they are four weeks old, they are transferred to the release site, a high place — a tower or cliff — to which, it is hoped, they will eventually return to nest. At this stage of the experiment, they are still in their natal down, but with some black feathers showing.

At the release site they are kept in nesting boxes (for protection from predators), and are fed until they learn to hunt. At about seven weeks the young birds can fly; at nine weeks the young birds begin to kill for themselves.

The release experiments began in the spring of 1975 at five release sites in the eastern United States. Three sites were man-made, two were natural, but all had two characteristics in common — a local abundance of natural prey and inaccessibility to human interference.

The two natural sites were known to be former eyries — one near Ithaca, the other on a cliff in the mountains near New Paltz, New York. The artificial sites were on platforms — one a former missile site at Drumlin Farm in Lincoln, Massachusetts, another on a coastal island in New Jersey, and the third, a seventy-five foot gunnery tower on Carroll Island, twenty miles northeast of Baltimore, amid miles of marsh and meadow. The Carroll Island release took place on June 3, 1975. It was much publicized by the press and television. Here is what happened:

Four four-week-old birds, one male and three females, were placed on the tower and fed. After two weeks they were released, with tiny transmitters attached to their legs. Within a few days they were chasing small birds and attempting rather ineffectual stoops. Early in July, feeding was stopped, and blindfolded pigeons were released. The peregrines responded as hoped — they made their first kill. In the following days, young green herons, crows, blue jays, and blackbirds were taken, and, by the end of July, all four had wandered far from Carroll Island. On July 30, one was seen perching on a window ledge of an office building in Baltimore; two weeks later, another was seen near Annapolis; two others were seen near grain elevators in Baltimore.

Most young peregrines released at the other sites also survived, and disappeared. Two were found dead at an early age, apparently the victims of great horned owls. One was recaptured and returned to Cornell. Of the sixteen released, twelve appeared to be self-supporting.

The 1975 program was to be a pilot scheme only — to test theory under reasonably natural conditions. To that extent, it was successful. But to repopulate the east with a hundred and fifty breeding pairs of wild peregrines, two hundred and fifty birds will have to be released every year for the next twenty years — not an easy task. Moreover, it will be at least 1978 before we know if any of the young have survived to breed, and, indeed, whether they will breed, for they will not reach sexual maturity until then.

Since all the young now being released come from eggs of tundra peregrines, perhaps they will return to the arctic when ready to nest. In their natural environment, they get twenty-four hours of daylight during the mating season; perhaps this is what they need. Traditionally, they are migrators; perhaps this urge will persist.

THE FUTURE

If they do migrate, and if they winter in South America, the luckless birds will again be exposed to a dangerous level of DDT poisoning. Most authorities believe that the tundra race, which still has several thousand members, is quickly disappearing, and may already be doomed. As we said at the beginning, the Peal's peregrine is much less affected by DDT. Living as it does in the Aleutians and Queen Charlottes where levels of egg contamination are still acceptable, the population is stable. Also, this group is less migratory. For these reasons, the Peal's eggs are now used to breed released stock. Releases of young from Peal's stock started in the east in 1976, with the hope that this stock will be less likely to migrate to South America.

Despite success in these areas, another danger exists. What if the released birds imprint on humans, exposed as they are to human association? There are many, many people who still hate birds of prey — the human-imprinted peregrines could easily fall victim to their careless destruction.

Attwater's Prairie Chicken

(Tympanuchus cupido attwateri)

North of the Mexican border are some twenty-one species of chicken-like land birds. They range in size from the three-foot-long turkey to the seven-inch harlequin quail and include five species of grouse, three ptarmigan, six quail, three introduced species (two partridge and a pheasant), and two full species of prairie chicken. All feed mostly on the ground. They prefer to walk or run unless flushed suddenly, and, when they fly, it is usually only for a short distance. They are largely non-migratory, although some move out of the northernmost part of their range in winter — for example, the ptarmigan.

Prairie chickens are large brown birds, about fourteen inches long, an average male weighing slightly more than two pounds. Females weigh about one and a half pounds. The back and underside are barred, with alternate darker and lighter stripes. The underside is much paler than the back; the wings are rounded, less distinctly barred than the body; the short tail is rounded and dark. The male Attwater's has an orange comb above the eye and an area of orange skin on each side of the neck. This orange neck area is inflated during courtship display and is beautiful to see. Tufts of feathers extending down each side of the neck, either parallel to the ground or elevated over the head, are also prominent during the display.

To repeat, there are two full species of prairie chickens — the greater prairie chicken (*Tympanuchus cupido pinnatus*) and the lesser prairie chicken (*Tympanuchus pallidicinctus*). Attwater's prairie chicken (*Tympanuchus cupido attwateri*) is a subspecies of the greater prairie chicken. These birds of the grasslands and unbroken prairies are in serious trouble. Cattle grazing, crop farming, and shooting have drastically reduced both their range and number.

HISTORY

The lesser prairie chicken is found only in the dry areas of the central United States, eastern New Mexico, northern Texas, and northeastern Oklahoma. In this restricted area, it manages to maintain a small population (which, because of poor habitat, was probably never large).

The greater prairie chicken and its subspecies, Attwater's prairie chicken are both listed as endangered. The greater prairie chicken once bred in the United States across the central and northern prairies; in Canada, from Alberta eastward to Manitoulin Island in Ontario. This range, once virtually continuous open grassland, is now limited to separate patches in northeastern Colorado, northwestern Kansas, Oklahoma, and eastward to northern Michigan. As a result, the greater prairie chicken is localized and rare, although some states are trying hard to re-establish it by purchasing land for its protection, by limiting cattle grazing on new reserves, and by improving habitat. Prairie chickens are now protected from hunting. Despite these measures, the greater prairie chicken's future remains precarious.

The heath hen (*Tympanuchus cupido cupido*), the prairie chicken of the east, could not withstand the shooting or the pressure on its habitat. In 1932, on Martha's Vineyard, the last bird died. Its fate is described on page 19. The heath hen and Attwater's prairie chicken are so closely related that most authorities classify them as the same species, but Attwater's is the southern race, limited to a belt close to the south Texas coast.

The greater prairie chicken and Attwater's prairie chicken have both suffered the same fate and for the same reasons; we have chosen to tell the Attwater's story because its range is more concentrated. Thus, its habits are better known.

LIFE CYCLE

The breeding cycle begins in late January when males congregate on their breeding or "booming" grounds, usually one-acre areas of short grass surrounded by heavy grasses with some brush cover for nesting. Here, in the early morning and evening, male birds congregate in groups of about a dozen, squabbling and bickering for favored locations. This goes on for about three weeks until the first females appear. Now follows a period of much foot stomping and booming. Booming is described as a *whur-zu-rrr* sound, but has many variations. It can sometimes be heard a mile away. In earlier times, settlers, surrounded by thousands of chickens, became thoroughly fed up with hearing it day after day. Val W. Lehmann, the leading authority on the Attwater's, describes the courtship behaviour:

> The appearance of the male, while booming, is striking. As a preliminary to uttering the call, he stretches his neck forward parallel to the ground. The erect... neck tufts point forward; the spread tail is held vertically or even inclined slightly over the back. The wings are extended downward and held firmly against the body and legs, the primaries almost touching the ground. The whole body appears strained and rigid. A short run forward is followed by vigorous stomping of the feet, which lasts only a few moments, but which under favorable conditions is distinctly audible for fifty feet or more. Inflation of the air sacs... is

synchronized with the stomping. The first syllable of the booming is given before the stomping ends, the male quickly jerking his head downward as he begins the call and keeping it there until the sac is deflated.

Hens visit the courtship grounds from March until the end of May. The peak of activity is in March. Pairing does not take place: prairie chickens are promiscuous. During their visits, the demure hens pay little attention to the fighting and posturing males. It is surprising then, that during a visit of only a few minutes, copulation may take place with one or several males.

Fighting is an important part of the male's sexual activity, possibly as a method of releasing surplus energy. Again, to quote Mr. Lehmann:

> Opponents usually approach each other, uttering peculiar whining notes, with necks outstretched, ear tufts erected, tails spread, wings drooped, and air sacs deflated. Then, as if possessed by the same thought, they suddenly hop off the ground, wings beating rapidly, and clash in midair. These bouts are usually discontinued after three or four flurries, and the victors seem satisfied after pursuing their opponents for short distances. Many feathers are frequently lost, but fights seldom end fatally. Males sometimes engage fancied opponents, as clumps of weeds or tufts of tall grass, and at other times they joust and bluff for periods up to thirty minutes or more without striking a blow . . . .

Hens make their own nests, incubate their eggs alone, and feed and protect their young. Nests are made within half a mile of the courtship ground, usually within a few feet of a trail or open area, almost invariably in grassy cover. The hen lays one egg each morning, until the clutch (which varies between eight and fifteen eggs) is complete. The nest is otherwise unattended until incubation. Incubation starts after the last egg has been laid.

While incubating, the hen is attentive, leaving the nest only twice a day to feed. After twenty-three or twenty-four days,

Attwater's prairie chicken ▶

hatching starts. It takes up to forty-eight hours for all the young to hatch. Within a few hours of hatching, the young are ready to leave the nest to begin feeding. This is a particularly

vulnerable time. The hatched young move in and out of the nest; odors are particularly strong and attract predators. For the first two weeks the hens brood their young at intervals during the day and all night. The chicks fly short distances at two weeks of age; at six to eight weeks the family breaks up.

THE DECLINE

Before settlers moved in, Attwater's prairie chicken occupied a continuous area from Louisiana to the Rio Grande, along three hundred miles of coast and up to a hundred miles inland. Most of this area was a combination of prairie, grassland with some trees, rivers, and much standing water. In all, some six million acres once housed hundreds of thousands of birds. By 1937, when Val W. Lehmann made his first study, the area had been reduced to 457,000 acres; the population to 8,700 birds. In 1967, after he had made another thorough survey, the area had shrunk to 234,000 acres and the population to 1,070 birds. It became clear that Attwater's prairie chicken was traveling on a fast road to extinction; unless some land was set aside for its use, its days were numbered. From eleven breeding areas in 1937, the number was reduced to two in 1967.

There are many causes for the decline, both natural and imposed. Natural causes — floods, droughts, hurricanes, hailstorms, and disease are no worse today than in the days before settlement. In those days, the prairie chicken was able to maintain itself because of its wide distribution.

What, then, is the real reason for the decline? It is the impact of imposed conditions: agriculture, pasture burning and mowing, overgrazing, oil development, drainage, shooting, urban development, and an increase in predation. Let us examine these culprits in more detail.

Where once there were over six million acres of useful habitat, only 250,000 are left — enough, however, to insure survival, if effectively managed.

Rice farming has taken over millions of acres. This intensive form of agriculture eliminates the prairie habitat. With few exceptions, rice fields are not left fallow long enough for suitable cover to grow. In one area of thirty thousand acres, there were some ten thousand birds in 1924, a year before rice farming began. By 1937, only one hundred and fifty were left.

Dry-land farming — cattle, peanuts, hay, and corn — is tolerated, provided some portions remain undisturbed.

In the coastal areas of Texas, the Indians and the early settlers set fires to burn off old grass to encourage new growth in the spring, and to control the growth of woody brush. They did this extensively and regularly. How did the fires affect the prairie chicken? The effects were mixed. Adult birds escaped easily; obviously eggs and chicks did not. Most burning was done before nesting began. Afterwards, little breeding cover remained, except on unsuitable, low ground. The burning was eventually stopped and there was, of course, an increase in brush cover, which reduced the usefulness of the land both for cattle grazing and for prairie chickens. (Today, brush-shredding machines and chemicals do the work of fires.)

Overgrazing is another problem. It reduces the cover, encourages the growth of unsuitable grasses and brush, and causes erosion. Reasonably controlled grazing does not seriously bother the prairie chicken; overgrazed land is useless.

In many areas, drainage has reduced the amount of standing water. Standing water is essential to the growth of cover, particularly during a drought. Many ponds, which used to support a rich surrounding plant life, have disappeared, eliminating much of the cover. (A protective cover is important for shade during the hot summer.)

Oil rigs and urban development have taken over some of the best prairie chicken habitat. The city of Houston, for example, covers nearly 300,000 acres. Unfortunately, some of these acres were once the finest habitat.

Predation has always been a factor in the prairie chicken range — crowded conditions have increased it enormously. Opossums, skunks, red wolves, raccoons, snakes are the chicken's natural enemies. Today, feral hogs, cats, and dogs have been added to the list. In the 1930s, it was profitable for farmers to trap fur-bearing animals, limiting the chicken's predators. It is no longer. (In today's range there are more predators than prairie chickens.)

Until 1883 the prairie chicken received no protection from hunters. In that year, the season was reduced from twelve to seven months, without however, a bag limit. In 1903, the season was reduced to three months, with a daily bag limit of twenty-five. (The new law was enforced by six wardens for the whole state of Texas!) In 1929, the season was reduced to four days with a limit of ten birds; and the number of wardens had been increased to nine. As transportation and roads improved, and the number of hunters increased, hunting laws became meaningless, as the following ugly story illustrates.

Between July and January in the early 1930s, organized groups would camp in likely areas, each hunter competing for the most birds killed. At the end of an encampment, the member of the group with the fewest birds paid the expenses of the others. Taking what they wanted, hundreds of birds were left for the vultures.

From 1916 until his death in 1931, H.P. Attwater, for whom this prairie chicken was renamed (from Bendire's), struggled for the birds. In 1937, six years after his death, legal protection became complete — there was to be no more open season on Attwater's.

Another man who has devoted himself to the survival of Attwater's prairie chicken is Val W. Lehmann. For forty years, he has worked towards this goal. Since 1937, when he was a young biologist with the Department of the Interior, he has studied the bird. His first treatise was published in 1941 and his work has continued ever since. In 1945, he left government service for wildlife management on the vast King Ranch in Texas. Here, his interest and that of his employers have led to more useful research.

THE FUTURE

In September, 1967, a hurricane dropped up to twenty-eight inches of rain and caused extensive flooding in Texas. In the western end of the range, the bird population dropped from fifteen hundred to two hundred and fifty — leaving only one thousand and seventy birds in existence.

In November of that year, representatives of the Texas and federal governments met with officials of Texas A & M University, the World Wildlife Fund, and other conservation organizations. The result — a survival plan. Since then, much has been accomplished: birds captured near the Ellington Air Force Base as a hazard to aircraft have been released in other areas, some retained for propagation in captivity. Ecological studies have been undertaken. Thousands of acres have been purchased and fenced. Cattle grazing has been reduced.

The results are promising. The population is beginning to grow. In 1975, the American Ornithologists' Union reported that aerial counts of males on booming grounds indicated a total population of about twenty-four hundred, the increase probably due to favorable weather for breeding. The American Ornithologists' Union reports there are now small, separate populations in twelve Texas counties, but warns that available prairie is sure to decline with ever-intensifying agricultural operations.

On the other hand, in 1971, Lehmann, encouraged by the reductions of government subsidies to rice growers, noted that less land producing rice means more land which can produce prairie chickens, and new management techniques (prescribed burning to improve habitat, impounding water, creating booming grounds, enhancing the food supply) spell hope. However, there has been one major stumbling block — the failure to produce young in captivity.

In 1971, Lehmann wrote: "It is heartening to know that concerted effort, at long last, is being exerted on the chicken's behalf. As Professor Attwater observed so many years ago, it is still possible to save the coastal prairie chicken — but only if a concerned public insists that this be done."

Masked
Bobwhite Quail

(Colinus virginianus ridgwayi)

For most of the year it is a hot, dry, land: in summer, the average temperature is 95° Fahrenheit and 105° Fahrenheit days are not uncommon; in winter, the average temperature is above freezing, but can sometimes dip below. During May and June humidity increases; in July the rain comes and continues intermittently until September. Some ten inches fall between July and September — but only three inches during the rest of the year. With the rains the land comes alive: the ground turns green, trees break into leaf, and the air buzzes with insects. Another inch of rain usually falls in December; after that there is almost none until June. The ground parches, grasses and leaves wither, and insects disappear. This is the habitat of the masked bobwhite quail (*Colinus virginianus ridgwayi*).

Bobwhite quail receive their name from their distinctive call. It is in two or three parts, a whistled *bob - bob - white*. The final note slurs upward. The widespread common bobwhite is an eight-inch long, reddish-brown bird with a short, stubby tail and wide, rounded wings. The underside is pale and barred, and there are brown on white spots on the flanks. The face is white, the crown dark, continuing in a line down the back of the neck. There is a dark line curving downward from behind the eye and around the neck to form a collar. The female is similarly marked, but the face is yellow instead of white.

The masked bobwhite, by contrast, is robin-red below; the face is black with a white streak above the eye and sometimes on the throat.

The bobwhite quail family is widely distributed through the eastern and midwestern United States and in much of southern Mexico; the masked bobwhite is a subspecies, with a much more restricted range — before 1900 it bred in a narrow band southward from Tucson, through Arizona and the Mexican state of Sonora almost to the Gulf of California coast at Guaymas.

In this area of mesquite grassland, the masked bobwhite was separated by several hundred miles to the south and across the Sierra Madre mountains to the east from other bobwhite populations — which is why the masked subspecies evolved. It did, however, share this range with four other quail species — Gambel's (*Lophcytyx gambelii*), the scaled quail (*Dallipepla squamata*), the elegant quail (*Lophortyx douglasii*), and Mearn's (*Cyrtonyx montezumae*); all more common and widely distributed than the masked bobwhite.

HISTORY

By 1900, the masked bobwhite was gone from Arizona, and a few years later from most of its Mexican range as well. Where a hundred years ago this little quail was reasonably prevalent, today it is vanishing because of overgrazing by cattle.

Before cattle invaded the bird's semi-arid range, it was covered with many varieties of annual grasses and weeds, with little brush, and, in the water courses, with trees. The bobwhite did quite well then — and it could probably even have tolerated a moderate amount of grazing.

Unfortunately, every part of the masked bobwhite's range has been overgrazed; a situation not apparent to the casual

Masked bobwhite quail ▶

visitor to the area, where one can drive for miles without seeing one cow; but it doesn't take many to eat the sparse grass to the ground, leaving little food for birds and other animals. When all grass has been eaten, nesting cover disappears and woody plant species take over. Eventually the open spaces with their waving grasses disappear, and a continuous cover of brush replaces them. The bobwhite has not been able to tolerate these new conditions; it has disappeared from most of its former territory. It lived on in Sonora because there ranching came later, mainly after 1940.

A verbal account reported by R.E. Tomlinson to the North American Wildlife Conference in 1972, recalls that the Sonora countryside in 1931 consisted of wide, grass-covered valleys in which some grasses reached over the heads of grazing deer. Twenty years later, the same area was bare; by 1970 it was entirely covered with brush. Brush burning has not been tried, but in some parts of Sonora an attempt *has* been made to revert the land back to grass by bulldozing the brush, leaving it in long rows. It was in these cleared areas, that the masked bobwhite might have had a chance to recover.

WHAT IS BEING DONE?

Twenty years ago it was thought that the bird was already extinct. In 1964, it was rediscovered on Benjamin Hill in Sonora. Biologist Stephen Galliziolo and taxidermists Seymour and James Levy from Tucson found the bird — the first sighting in fourteen years.

The Levys had earlier attempted to raise masked bobwhites in captivity for release in Arizona, but their experiment could not be tested because vandals broke into the birds' pens and killed most of them. The Levys donated the remaining four pairs to the then Bureau of Sport Fisheries and Wildlife. In 1967, R.E. Tomlinson of the Bureau was commissioned to undertake a study to determine the distribution, limiting factors, and overall status of the masked bobwhite.

But first, the birds had to be found. For nearly three years, Tomlinson and his team searched out the elusive quail. Hundreds of Mexican cowboys, ranch owners, and villagers were interviewed. Each was shown a card with pictures of all the quail species and asked which, if any, were familiar.

During the summers when the males were calling their "bobwhite" call, the investigators traveled the range and played recorded female calls as a decoy. During the winters, they searched with dogs. Even the nests of wrens and verdins, which are partially built of bird feathers, were opened and searched for bobwhite feathers. Eight separate former ranges were demarcated and searched.

The results? Only in the area of Benjamin Hill, where the birds were first rediscovered, was there a population large enough to be studied effectively. Eventually more than a thousand birds were counted here. Here the team obtained the landowner's permission — and interest — to carry out the survey. By that time (1967) brush had already been cleared from ten thousand acres, and much of the land had reverted to the desired vegetation — grass. They established a weather station to measure rainfall, humidity, and temperature extremes; and they fixed on a twenty-mile weekly route to count bobwhite calls during the mating season.

The team's research proved productive immediately. First, they learned a lot about the bird: mating does not begin until the rains come in early July; nesting success is higher in the wetter summers; incubation peaks between August 10 and 24; the broods appear late in September; the masked bobwhite is as productive as other quail subspecies — it produces broods of five to fifteen young, with an average of eleven; autumn coveys are essentially family groups, but unproductive adults and strays join them, hence early coveys consist of about twelve birds.

Between 1968 and 1971, Tomlinson undertook banding and trapping, which captured a total of 183 birds. Fifty-seven were shipped to the Patuxent Wildlife Research Center in Laurel, Maryland, for propagation in captivity; the rest were released. Evidence obtained from the trapping program indicated that annual mortality, even without shooting, is about sixty-five percent; in other words, it is extremely high.

The bobwhites shipped to Patuxent did well. Between 1970 and 1976, about 3,600 captive bred birds were sent to Arizona and released.

The story, however, does not end here, nor does it have a happy ending. A century of overgrazing in Arizona has modified the range to such an extent that even in the best of the habitat, insufficient cover and food remain. The release program is being wound down—there is simply no suitable refuge where the birds have a chance to survive. Captive stock, however, will be maintained in case some day enough habitat can be restored to attempt further reintroduction.

In Mexico, the situation has deteriorated to such an extent since 1970 that the small population in Sonora will probably be gone within a few years. Overgrazing has again been the cause, and the masked bobwhite's outlook is bleak.

Whooping Crane

(*Grus americana*)

Cranes are beautiful — pure white bodies and tails, black wingtips, long black legs, bare bright red crowns, and black mustaches. They stand five feet high, have a wingspan of nearly eight feet, and weigh about twenty pounds. Young birds, three months old, are as large as their parents and a mottled pink-brown. In flight the neck and legs are outstretched. Their wild bugling call can be heard two miles away; the call is made only while in the nesting territory and in winter, but not in flight.

The whooping crane, like the California condor, is a relict from the Pleistocene period. Fossils found in Idaho are from birds which lived about 3,500,000 years ago, and are identical to the bones of the modern bird. In pre-historic times, it ranged west to California and east to Kentucky — how numerous, no one knows.

THE DECLINE

The story of how the whooping crane came to the brink of extinction is typical of other birds requiring large spaces to live. Until about 1850, it wintered in suitable southern marshes from the Atlantic to western Mexico and nested in Illinois, Iowa, Minnesota, North Dakota, Manitoba, Saskatchewan, and Alberta, and, presumably, in the Northwest Territories where its only present breeding area was discovered in 1954. The total population was not large even then — probably under two thousand. Much has been made of the large numbers shot indiscriminately for food or for the sake of killing when the prairies were first settled. Today's numbers, however, would not be much different, even without this earlier slaughter. Why? The problem is one of getting enough space both for nesting and for winter feeding. Settlement of the North American prairies (where the bird nested), inevitably led to draining marshes for crops and pasture, thus eliminating huge areas of former range. Since each pair will not nest without an undisturbed marsh area of about a thousand acres in summer and four to six hundred acres for winter feeding, as far as nesting in the United States was concerned, the bird was excluded as early as 1889, when the last nest was found. In Saskatchewan nesting continued until 1922. Today the only nesting site is in the Northwest Territories, fortunately in the protected Wood Buffalo National Park.

LIFE CYCLE

No North American bird receives as much publicity or generates as much interest as the whooping crane — its progress on spring and autumn migrations is reported in the press almost daily. From late November to early December, all the birds arrive from the north at their only remaining natural wintering area, the Aransas National Wildlife Refuge on the Texas coast. Here, they feed for most of the day on crabs, clams, mud shrimp, frogs, and crayfish. Parents continue to feed their young of the year, although by this time, the young bird is six months old and capable of looking after itself.

Territorial demands of each pair or family group are strong. At Aransas and in the islands near the refuge, the earliest arrivals claim the best areas, excluding their own kind, but tolerating other birds and animals. It is here that biologists make the final count of new birds for that year and of survivors

of previous years. In the autumn of 1976, the total population of wild and captive birds was ninety-nine. The perils of the twenty-five-hundred-mile flight from north of the 60th Parallel to Texas are many. (In 1976, one bird died because it was caught in a fence.)

The Texas refuge covers some forty-seven thousand acres. Unfortunately, only about five thousand acres are suitable for feeding. This acreage is claimed by family groups with their usually single young, and provides space for only about ten pairs. Unmated birds — those too young to breed and older, unattached birds — feed where they can, usually at the edge of the established territories and on Matagorda and St. Joseph Islands. Here, however, even the present few are crowded, for the marshes on these islands are narrow. Natural or man-caused disasters from hurricanes to oil spills could finish off this small wild population, living as it does in a relatively small and exposed area for about five months of the year. A tragic precedent is the fate which overtook the now-extinct Louisiana flock: it was reduced from thirteen to six in a disastrous hurricane in 1940, and had disappeared entirely by 1949.

Pairs mate for life. The young of the previous year is less welcome in late winter when the courtship process starts. It may even be driven off for a period. The young bird does, however, rejoin its parents for the dramatic flight north. Territorial defences are abandoned in late March and small groups start to form in readiness for migration. Migration is in an almost straight line to the northwest — through Texas, Oklahoma, Kansas, Nebraska, South and North Dakota, Saskatchewan, and Alberta. The whooping crane's destination, which it reaches some time in April, is an area in Wood Buffalo National Park, north of the 60th Parallel in the Northwest Territories and south of Great Slave Lake. Here, in a land of ponds, rivers, and muskeg, the survivors arrive, after flying twenty-five hundred miles in fifteen or sixteen days. It is interesting to note that before the end of the journey the young of the previous year leave their parents to seek their own life for the next five years, at which time they reach sexual maturity and mate.

Sixteen is the maximum number of pairs observed on the nesting ground in two of the last ten years, which means that twenty to twenty-five birds summer elsewhere. Where exactly,

nobody knows. Pairs appear to return to the same general area each year, sometimes to the same pond, but never to the same nest site. The park's pothole tundra is poorly drained, but provides enough solid ground to support black spruce, tamarack, willow, and dwarf birch. Nesting sites are on islands in the many small lakes of the area or along their shores, where there is a heavy cover of bulrushes. The nest is on a mound of bulrushes usually in shallow water, in an area which the pair has cleared. Two eggs and occasionally three are laid, two days apart. Incubation is shared by both birds and lasts for thirty-four or thirty-five days. During this time, one bird stands on guard and feeds on insects, mollusks, and fish. The young hatch during the first week of June, but rarely do both eggs hatch, probably because of the staggered laying. When they do, one chick usually dies. The robin-sized downy young is able to run about after the first day, but returns to the nest at night for two or three weeks. It is capable of flight after about two months, well in time for the southward migration, which gets under way by the third week of September. This flight is more leisurely than the spring migration — the last birds do not arrive in Aransas until late November or early December.

THE FUTURE

The nesting area *must* not be tampered with, if this last remnant group of cranes is to survive. Some years ago, a proposal to build a railway to service the base-metal deposits at Pine Point, if implemented, would have taken the railway line within ten miles downstream of the Sass-Nyarling nesting area. Luckily, the idea has been scrapped, but more recent proposals to build an electric transmission line and two microwave towers within a few miles of the nearest nest have been put forward. Conservationists are often accused of scare tactics, an accusation which is sometimes justified; their efforts on behalf of the crane, however, have been enormous, and their recommendations must be heeded if the crane is to survive.

Until 1954, when the world's only breeding area was discovered, it was impossible to do anything to help the crane except to protect the wintering ground. From 1941, when the population reached a low of fifteen, it gradually increased to forty-three in 1964. During the late 1950s, plans to capture the whole flock, and try to build it up in captivity for gradual release to the wild were considered too drastic and were scrapped. In 1964, the then United States Bureau of Sport Fisheries and Wild Life and the Canadian Wildlife Service decided to take a number of eggs from nesting cranes in Wood Buffalo National Park for hatching and propagation at the Patuxent Center for Endangered Wildlife Research in Maryland. The biologists working on this project knew that, although two eggs are laid, in the twenty-four years since 1940, of the 103 young cranes which had arrived in Texas, only eight had been twins. It was considered reasonable, therefore, to take one egg from each nest a few days before hatching. Two years of careful planning and research followed. Nests were found by aerial observation. By May 28, 1969, nine had been located and the first airlift took place.

Ernest Kuyt, a biologist with the Canadian Wildlife Service, was chosen to get the eggs. He had spent the previous two summers studying cranes and he knew their habits and habitat better than anyone else. The plan involved two trips by helicopter from Fort Smith — the second to insure that not all eggs would be lost in case the helicopter crashed on the first trip. A higher-flying fixed-wing aircraft monitored the behavior of the parent birds. Eggs were kept warm in a suitcase fitted with hot-water bottles. All went well, until it was realized that Kuyt had forgotten to bring a specially fitted box to carry the egg from the nest to the waiting helicopter. He solved this problem by carrying the eggs in spare heavy socks (he used socks in all subsequent years). Using a stick for support, he waded to the nest (the parent bird having taken flight), picked up one egg, and carried it carefully to the helicopter, after having photographed and measured the nest. The first pickup took thirteen minutes; eventually the time was reduced to nine. To everybody's relief, the parents soon returned to the nest and resumed incubation of the remaining egg.

In this way eggs were collected and sent to the Patuxent Research Center in 1967, 1968, 1969, 1971, and 1974 — fifty eggs in all. Hatching success there has been better than in the wild: nineteen birds have been raised. It is, however, too early to know if this experiment has been successful, as these birds have not yet reproduced. Historically, mating captive cranes has been a problem.

Another experiment, undertaken in 1973, aims to establish a second breeding colony geographically removed from the Aransas–Wood Buffalo flock. If successful, this colony will reduce the hazard of a wipe-out such as the Louisiana wipe-out of the 1940s. The plan involves replacement of the eggs of wild greater sandhill cranes nesting in Gray's Lake National Wildlife Refuge in Idaho, with those of whooping cranes taken from the Wood Buffalo National Park. The greater sandhill crane (*Grus canadensis tabida*) is a rare southern subspecies of the smaller sandhill crane (*Grus canadensis*). In size, it is similar to the whooping crane, but it is gray-brown with a red patch on the forepart of its head. Earlier research indicates that the greater sandhill will accept the alien egg in place of its own, and that it will raise the young whooping crane as its own. It is hoped that the young will migrate with the sandhills to their wintering refuges in Colorado and New Mexico, returning in the spring to Idaho.

On May 28, 1975, fourteen eggs were taken and flown by Ernie Kuyt to Fort Smith, and on the following day by a chartered aircraft to Idaho Falls. Atmospheric pressure inside the planes was kept at ground level and oxygen was introduced regularly into the portable incubator. From Idaho Falls the eggs flew by helicopter to Gray's Lake, where they were placed on the nests of their pre-selected foster parents. The results? Of the fourteen, nine eggs hatched, two were lost to predators, and three proved to be infertile.

During the winter of 1976, four young whooping cranes were sited in a refuge in New Mexico, and, in the autumn of 1976, young whoopers were observed in the sandhill flock in New Mexico on the day before the open season on sandhills began. But here lies another threat — as long as shooting of sandhills is permitted, the young foster whooping cranes are endangered.

How have the whooping cranes of Wood Buffalo National Park reacted to man's interference? The good news is that there have been no negative effects. Indeed, the rate of breeding survival has increased, because of the efforts of the governments of the United States and Canada and private organizations such as the National Audubon Society. Numbers (in the wild) have risen to about sixty from a low of fifteen: they may well remain at this level because of the lack of suitable winter habitat unless the Gray's Lake group starts to breed. The odd bird is still lost to thoughtless gunners and through accident on migration — the balance between survival and extinction remains precarious.

Eskimo Curlew

(Numenius borealis)

Fossil remains indicate the Eskimo curlew has been around for more than 200,000 years, and as late as the 1830s was so numerous that John James Audubon compared its vast flocks with the passenger pigeon's.

Now it is almost gone, its breeding grounds unknown.

The Eskimo is the smallest North American curlew. It measures about thirteen inches. In the field it is almost indistinguishable from the whimbrel which is, however, larger, with a longer, more down-curved bill. Brown and somewhat speckled on the back, the Eskimo has a whitish face, marked with a dark, indistinctly striped crown, mottled breast, and pale abdomen. It is so like the little whimbrel of Siberia (*Numenius minutus*), which migrates to the East Indies and northern Australia, that some authorities insist the two are the same species.

LIFE CYCLE

This little curlew's story is best told by following it on its annual migration route, using evidence recorded since the bird's first discovery by white men in 1772. In that year, traders of the Hudson Bay Company at Fort Albany in James

Bay and Fort Severn in Hudson Bay sent specimens to London. Samuel Hearne, the great lone explorer of the Coppermine, recorded the bird in his journal. On June 13, 1822, Dr. John Richardson, a member of Sir John Franklin's first expedition in search of a northwest passage, found the first nest — at Point Lake on the Coppermine River. Between 1822 and 1865, when the last nest was found, the breeding area was established to be westward across the Northwest Territories from the Coppermine and probably included Alaska, because many birds were seen there in the spring.

In late May, the birds arrived in the north from South America. They must have nested immediately after arrival, because they were already in Labrador before the end of July — on their way south. The breeding ground itself was on the tundra close to the Arctic Ocean. Here the curlew laid three or four eggs in a nest built of leaves and dead grass, located in hollows.

In the summer of 1833, Audubon watched vast flocks at Bras d'Or Harbor in Labrador. The following year, he published one of his finest plates of the Eskimo curlew — prophetically showing one bird lying dead.

As soon as the young were old enough to undertake the long migration, they started eastward across northern North America to the coast of Labrador. (Not all followed this route; birds were also sighted in Ontario, Illinois, and Ohio.) In Labrador, flocks rested and fed for some time in preparation for the long journey south. They fed largely on crowberries, plentiful in Labrador and Alaska. They probably also took insects and snails, as they did in the spring. In Labrador, the birds put on weight and fat. They had to: they lost one-fifth of their weight in the non-stop twenty-five-hundred-mile flight to South America.

We know little of the route south. It appeared to be east of Bermuda and past Barbados with land-fall from the Guianas to Brazil. Not all the birds flew non-stop. Some stopped in

Newfoundland and Nova Scotia, and, in one account from 1863, more than seven thousand birds were shot in one day on Nantucket Island. In 1888, large numbers were seen flying past the Barbados, and, of the few which landed, one man shot more than a hundred. There are other early accounts of exhausted birds arriving as far off course as Ireland and Scotland and at unusual points on the American coast. Storms must have accounted for many of these landings.

From available records, relatively few curlews have been seen from Bermuda to Barbados. Most flew without stopping from Labrador to South America; the journey took at least sixty hours. Although curlews could land on water, it did them little good for they would soon become saturated. In the air snow clogged their feathers, and strong winds drove them from their course. (Golden plovers appear to take the same route; they, however, start from farther south.)

Almost nothing is known of the route south through South America. In 1880, however, large flocks were reported in Uruguay as early as September 9, which indicates the route that year must have been direct, with few stops. Mid-October was the more usual time for arrival in Argentina. Here they spread out on the plains of Patagonia and southern Chile, feeding alone or with flocks of golden plovers.

By late February or early March, the flocks were on their way north again. Nothing is known of their route, except for a single specimen taken in Guatemala in April. Some ornithologists say the path was westward across the Andes and up the narrow Pacific shore; others that it was to the east of the Andes across the Amazon basin. What is known, however, is that by mid-March huge flocks arrived on the Texas and Louisiana coasts.

THE DECLINE

The Eskimo curlew proved hopelessly vulnerable to the market gunners with their shotguns. Each spring flocks moved east-

Eskimo curlew ▶

TMShortt.

ward along the Gulf coast to the Mississippi, joining the millions upon millions of other birds who use that northward flyway. From the 1850s until 1875, there appeared to be no lessening of numbers. They arrived faithfully in March, moving gradually northward, feeding and resting as they went, usually choosing to feed on newly plowed fields in which grubs and insects had been turned to the surface.

The shooting was ridiculously easy: the flocks flew in tight masses. Even then, one hunter complained: "... they generally fly in so loose and straggling a manner that it is rare to kill more than half a dozen birds at a shot. When they wheel, however, in any of their beautiful evolutions, they close together in a more compact body and offer a more favorable opportunity for the gunner."

Here was no question of sport, only of economy — to kill as many birds as possible with one shot. Often the numbers shot far exceeded the capacity of the wagons brought by the hunters to carry the slaughtered flocks, and huge piles of birds, thousands in number, were left to rot in the fields. Those that were carried away were sold in the markets throughout the midwest; great numbers were also sent east by rail.

After 1875, the decline became precipitous, although some flocks still came through and the shooting continued. Most gunners assumed they were having a bad year, and that the curlew was in another part of the country. The truth was they were nearly all gone. After 1883, curlews were not seen in Arkansas and Michigan; nor after 1884 in Oklahoma and South Dakota. So it went, state after state saw its last bird. In 1926, one was seen in Nebraska; since then they have been seen in the United States only on the Texas coast, where, as has been mentioned already, they occasionally turn up in ones and twos. It is, of course, possible that more do arrive but are not sighted. Interest in the Galveston area, however, is high, and many competent bird watchers vie for the chance to record a sighting.

We know nothing of the Eskimo curlew's life span; other curlew species, however, are known to be long-lived (over thirty years), and it is possible the few remaining Eskimo curlews are old ones. But since it has been eighty years since flocks have been seen, some nesting must have taken place. The breeding ground of the few remaining birds (if any) is unknown — the last nest was found over one hundred years ago; two birds were sighted in Martha's Vineyard in 1972. No more were seen until August 1976. That year, Archie Hagar, an experienced ornithologist, was participating in a shorebird banding program at North Point, a few miles from Moosonee, Ontario. There he sighted two Eskimo curlews, the first to be recorded in Ontario in more than a hundred years.

THE FUTURE

It is easy to blame the shotgun and the greedy hunter who fired it for this catastrophic decline, but it may not be the whole story. The perils of migration or disease may also have been factors; Eskimos may have found the nesting grounds — we shall never know.

Public interest along the Texas coast is high; if any more arrive they will almost certainly be seen by the hundreds of avid birders who search the flocks of feeding shore birds. Whether or not this will ever happen is doubtful. It is sad though safe to assume that the Eskimo curlew will soon be extinct.

For obvious reasons, active recovery efforts are impractical, and, since all curlews are protected from shooting, the Eskimo receives the same small comfort.

Hudsonian Godwit

(Limosa haemastica)

There is a certain irony in this story, and the joke is on us. Until 1942 the Hudsonian godwit was thought to be almost extinct; now we suspect it has been fairly common all along. How did this unassuming bird fool North American ornithologists, academics, and bird watchers for so long? It is an interesting story.

APPEARANCE

Hudsonian godwits are large shorebirds with long, slightly upturned bills. Their bills are flexible at the tip, enabling them to probe deep in mud for mollusks and insects. Their breeding plumage is a rich reddish brown below, with dark upper parts, white rump, and black tail. Winter plumage is gray. In flight the white rump and the dark tail distinguish the Hudsonian from the willet, which it resembles. The female is noticeably larger than the male.

Early literature wrongly describes the Hudsonian as the quietest of all shorebirds — on its breeding grounds, it is one of the noisiest.

HISTORY

In 1840, Audubon said it was "of rare occurrence in any part of the United States," and he never saw one alive. This did not stop the Hudsonian from being shot by hunters whenever it did appear — in spring on its migration northward through the Mississippi valley, and in autumn on its way to South America via the east coast. In 1927, A.C. Bent, in his *Life History* of this species, describes it as "now almost extinct."

Early information is patchy, but interesting. The first nest was discovered in the arctic at Fort Anderson on June 9, 1862; another on the lower Anderson River the same year. The nest consisted of "a few withered leaves placed in a hole or depression in the ground." (A.C. Bent in *Life History*.) In 1897, another nest was found in the Mackenzie Delta.

It was known the birds migrated in a southeasterly direction from the arctic, because, on August 24, 1900, they were sighted at Cape Churchill on Hudson Bay. Godwits were seldom seen in southern Canada and the inland states, but some autumn records do exist. On the east coast, they were seen more often on islands in the Gulf of St. Lawrence, in the Magdalen Islands, the Maritime Provinces, and along the United States coast south to Long Island — a few birds at a time. In the light of recent findings, these birds must have been stragglers, blown to shore by easterly and northeasterly storms.

Wherever they were seen, they were shot. In 1903, ornithologist Dr. L.C. Sanford describes a hunting trip to the Magdalen Islands:

> At high water they congregate on the upper beaches, well out of reach of any disturber. For a long time it was impossible to arrange a blind in the range of the flight, but finally, by piling up heaps of seaweed and stalking them down far out in the shallow water, we managed to kill a small number. They quickly learned the danger, however, and would keep on their course, just out of reach.

In 1920, Ernest Gibson, who provided much South American data to science, reports they were plentiful in the Province of Buenos Aires in Argentina — appearing in flocks of a thousand or more. He adds:

> On more than one of these occasions several birds dropped to my gun. The flock would then again and again sweep round and hover over the individuals in the water, uttering loud cries of distress, quite regardless of my presence in the open, and the renewed gunfire. Though the godwit is such an excellent table bird, I found myself unable to continue the slaughter under these circumstances. I might select my birds, but so closely were they packed together that the shots went practically 'into the brown' and caused innumerable cripples.

It is clear that only a small percentage of the total stopped on the east coast of North America, because far more birds were seen in South America than were thought to exist. Because only the occasional bird was sighted, it was assumed the Hudsonian godwit was almost extinct — a victim of early overshooting. Until 1942.

DISCOVERY

In the summer of 1942, world-famous bird artist Terence Shortt (whose beautiful pictures appear in this book) and C.E. Hope, his companion, were traveling in James Bay. They left Fort Albany on the west shore of the bay on July 15, canoed to the mouth of the Nettichi River, camped there for four days; then went on to Big Piskwanish Point where they camped for four more, arriving at Moosonee, Ontario, on July 25. Their journey intentionally coincided with the greatest concentration and early migration of the many species of shorebirds which nest in the tundra-forest country along the Hudson Bay coast. They saw huge flocks of whimbrels, knots, and sandpipers. Some had nested locally, others were early migrants from farther north.

They also saw the Hudsonian godwit: a bird thought to be almost extinct. They saw not one or two, but an estimated twelve-hundred birds — far more than had been seen in all of North America since 1900! In one period of an hour and a half, they counted a thousand, in flocks of sixty to seventy, all flying in a southeasterly direction.

THE SEARCH FOR NESTS

Long before Shortt and Hope made their discovery, P.A. Taverner and A.C. Lloyd, the Canadian ornithologists, had seen and collected spring specimens in Hudson Bay. They did not, however, find conclusive evidence of nesting.

Hudsonian godwit ▶

By 1930, the port of Churchill in Manitoba had made the western shore of Hudson Bay fairly accessible to naturalists. To establish a shorter export route to Europe for western grain, the railway north from Winnipeg was extended through the spruce forests and tundra, and the final five-hundred-mile section from The Pas, Manitoba to Churchill was completed in 1930. Taverner and Lloyd made the trip shortly after the completion of the railway. They found ten pairs of Hudsonian godwits, but no nests.

In 1947, Hazel R. Ellis, of the Department of Ornithology of Cornell University, went to Churchill for the prime purpose of finding the nest of the Hudsonian godwit — and did. The nest contained three eggs, which hatched on July 8, 1947. The find made her the first person to see the downy young.

In 1961, more nests were found by Leslie Tuck, the noted Canadian ornithologist, and, in 1962, J.A. Hagar began a study of Hudsonian godwit nesting in the Churchill area. For the next few years he was there for part of each summer. His study spanned the period from late May, when the ground is still snow covered, until late summer, when the last juveniles depart. Because of his work much more is now known about this bird.

LIFE CYCLE

The first godwits arrive in the Churchill area early in June. (Churchill is at the northern limit of heavy tree cover and near the southern limit of godwit nesting.) Godwits arrive in small flocks. They are preceded by larks, longspurs, and snow buntings, which are everywhere in the few snowless patches. Ducks and geese arrive next; a day or two later, the first sandpipers and godwits. Godwits arrive in small flocks of about a dozen birds. The flocks break up — some stay to nest, others push on farther north. The godwit's preferred nesting habitat is sedge marsh, an extensive grassy meadow near the tidal flats.

Nesting begins immediately on arrival and by mid-June the eggs have been laid — three or four in each nest. Incubation lasts for twenty-two or twenty-three days. The young hatch after the first week in July. Nesting success is high; in ten closely observed nests, thirty-six eggs produced thirty young.

Now begins a remarkable period of growth. All arctic nesting shorebirds must grow quickly if they are to be strong enough to endure the rigors of migration, and the Hudsonian godwit must grow even faster because it is larger than most, and has the longest migration flight.

The hatchling is a grotesque little thing — all feet. The middle toe is almost as large on hatching as it will ever be, but because the family remains in the nest for only a few hours after the last chick has hatched, the young must be dry and agile, able to run about through the grass; swim and find their own food. In the next thirty days growth is prodigious. Hatchlings grow to be almost as large as their parents; feathers replace down; the bill grows almost to its full length; and last, the bird learns to fly.

Parents guard their young during most of this thirty-day period, but do not feed them. Late in July parents desert (a few days before the young have learned to fly) and retire to the tidal marshes where, for the next month, they feed heavily. They are very thin and must gain strength for the migration ahead.

By July 23 the first migrating adults have moved far south of their breeding grounds. In the course of the next month other adults (those that did not breed that year) follow, and, by August 5, the now-fledged juveniles also start south.

By mid-August godwits from the northwestern and central arctic arrive at Hudson Bay. The whole population is now on the one shore — a narrow strip a mile or so wide and a thousand miles long. They begin to move southeastward down the coast, in stages, to southern James Bay, passing any given point at a rate of three to four thousand a day. By mid-August adults have started for South America; the young leave between September 15 and October 10.

THE MIGRATION

The 1942 discovery changed all the current hypotheses. Ornithologists rushed to adjust their theories. They assumed that godwits, on leaving the James Bay area, flew non-stop over the settled parts of Canada and the United States to remote and unobserved parts of South America. (Had they landed in any numbers on the eastern seaboard, the West Indies, the Antilles, or the north coast of South America, they would have been spotted long ago.) There is, however, one reference on October 10, 1878, from Barbados which notes, "This species passed over the island in large and almost continuous flocks the whole day." (Probably somewhat off their usual route.)

Assuming their course took them across Ontario and New England to the east coast, then southeast across the Atlantic close to Barbados to South America, the most probable touchdown points are the vast mud flats at the mouth of the Orinoco or Amazon — a distance of some 2,800 to 3,000 miles from Hudson Bay. This is the route (or one quite similar to it) of adult golden plovers. (Immature golden plovers follow an easier coastal route). This was also the route of the Eskimo curlew.

All godwits fly non-stop, whatever their age. Juveniles leave James Bay about a month later than adults, but even then they are only ten weeks removed from the egg.

The flight to South America takes about seventy-two hours, and to endure its rigors, the birds must be strong and rested. In early November they arrive in Argentina. Where have they been the preceding two months? Nobody knows for certain.

As mentioned above, it is thought they land in Brazil to feed on the vast mud flats of the Orinoco and the Amazon. Unfortunately, this area is desperately short of food, and it stands to reason the birds are in danger of being slaughtered.

We know little of the spring migration. It is thought to be through central and western South America to Texas and Louisiana, arriving there sometime in April. Groups spotted in Louisiana and Texas have invariably been small, an indication that large flocks break up before the start of the migration. This, of course, is an effective defense against hunters. Otherwise, the Hudsonian godwit would have been as vulnerable to spring shooting in the central plains as the Eskimo curlew once was.

This bird, thought to be practically extinct fifty years ago, found to be fairly common, and now suspected to have been common all along, was on the endangered species list for many years. It has now been removed from the endangered species list — and the Hudsonian godwit's story is one of the few stories in this book that has a happy ending.

Ivory-Billed Woodpecker

(*Campephilus principalis*)

The ivory-billed woodpecker is probably extinct. The last authenticated sighting was in 1952; there were unconfirmed reports in 1963 and 1966, a controversial photograph in 1971, and nothing since. This bird's plight is almost as well known as the condor's and the whooping crane's. Its enormous, almost-white bill, flaming red crest (of the male), and dramatic black and white wings and body are familiar to everybody even remotely interested in birds. Larger than a crow, it is the largest of the North American woodpeckers. In flight the white on the fore and after parts of the wing gives it a slender appearance, as, swooping and powerful, it flashes through the mature forest.

The call is similar to that of the tiny nuthatch — a *yank, yank* — only considerably louder. Much of the time, however, it is silent, and, when called, cannot be relied on to answer. But it can make a lot of noise, as the following story illustrates.

One day while on a trip through the southern states, Alexander Wilson shot an ivory-billed woodpecker. (Wilson was one of the greatest ornithologists of the nineteenth century; Audubon was a contemporary.)

The bird was only slightly wounded. Wilson caught it and put it in a bag, and "on being caught, (it) uttered a loudly reiterated, and most piteous note, exactly resembling the violent crying of a young child; which terrified my horse so, as

nearly to have cost me my life." When Wilson arrived in the next town, he attracted a lot of attention — people thought he had a child in his bag. Later in the day he took a room at an inn and left the bird there for a time. When he returned, the bird had smashed large holes in the plaster of the walls and ceiling, and when Wilson tethered it to his bed, it went to work on the legs, damaging them badly.

One can only guess at the ivory-bill population in Alexander Wilson's time. We know it was quite common because Audubon describes its habits in considerable detail (often inaccurately), but he does not appear to have had any problem finding birds to describe.

The range is in doubt too: some ornithologists said it nested from New Jersey to Mexico; Wilson doubted there were any north of Virginia. But whatever the range, it is likely that numbers were reasonably large in the southern states in swampy forests, particularly around the basin of the Mississippi River.

THE DECLINE

Nobody knows all the causes for the ivory-bill's (probable) extinction. By the time science had advanced to the stage where it could properly research the causes, there were not enough birds left to research. We do know the contributing factors — let us examine them in some detail by studying the bird's history, habitat, and what we know of its life cycle.

Human pressure has long been heavy — even before European settlement. Mark Catesby, the English explorer who first described the ivory-bill in 1731, wrote that "The bills of these Birds (*sic*) are much valued by the Canada Indians, who made coronets of 'em for their Princes and Great Warriors by fixing them round a wreath with points outward. The Northern Indians, having none of these Birds in their cold country, purchased them from the Southern People at the price of two, sometimes three, Buckskins a Bill." After European settlement shooting also took its toll, but probably did no more than temporary, local harm.

The real cause of first the decline, and then the probable extinction of the ivory-bill has been forest cutting.

To survive, ivory-bills require a great deal of uncut forest, because their only source of food comes from the forest — they need a steady diet of the larvae of the engraver beetle. This beetle eats a network of tracks just under the bark of a dead or dying tree. Woodpeckers attack the bark, tearing off large slabs and return again and again to the same tree until it is almost

Ivory-billed woodpecker ▶

bare of bark. Enough suitable trees to maintain ivory-bills occur only in large forest tracts.

Each pair of ivory-bills requires about two thousand acres of forest. By comparison, the slightly smaller, pileated wood-pecker (*Dryocopus pileatus*) has been able to adapt to small woodlots throughout its much larger range (which extends into southern Canada). The pileated feeds on carpenter ants (which tunnel through the heartwood of trees) by bashing out six-inch-oblong holes in the tree.

From about 1885 on, the logging industry in the south grew in leaps and bounds, with the result that the ivory-bill disap-peared rapidly and completely from many areas. By 1939 it lived on in only five separate locations in Louisiana, Florida, and eastern Texas — and the total population had plummeted to twenty-two birds.

The ivory-bill is essentially sedentary. When the forest in one area is destroyed, the local population tends to die off rather than move out. There are, however, exceptions: period-ically birds have been reported in new areas. By and large, though, their inability to adapt to smaller forests and move on has brought about their downfall.

LIFE CYCLE

The ivory-billed woodpecker was adaptable in one way. It did not require a specific kind of forest or tree — provided that the trees were large and the forest was regularly flooded and damp. In Florida, ivory-bills lived in a cypress swamp with the nest-hole cut into a live cypress. Here, they fed on larvae under the bark of fire-killed pines. Audubon wrote that "The hole is, I believe, always made in the trunk of a live tree, generally an ash or a hackberry, and it is at a great height." Other trees, such as dead oak and royal palm, were also used.

The hole in the tree was about five-by-four inches, usually thirty feet or more from the ground. It went straight into the tree for about five inches, then down two feet or more, ending in a jug-shaped cavity in which the nest was made.

Modern research into the life cycle and nesting habits of the ivory-bill is quite limited, for the opportunity came too late. But in the spring and summer of 1935, Dr. A.A. Allen, an eminent ornithologist from Cornell University, had an opportunity to study three nesting sites. (His account appears in *The Auk* of April, 1937.) For four days he and two assistants set up a camp, only a hundred yards from a tree where a pair of ivory-bills was nesting. They built a blind high in an adjacent tree thirty feet from the nest-hole, and there was considerable movement by the observers in and out of the blind.

In each of the three nests which Allen studied that summer, a clutch of eggs was laid and incubated, and the young hatched. In each case the nest-hole was abandoned within a few days of hatching. Dr. Allen does not mention his own group's disturbance as a possible cause of the abandonment, but this possibility must be considered. Even Audubon, writing more than a century earlier, describes the inability of the bird to accommodate itself to man's presence. He notes that ivory-bills abandon nests even when watched from a distance.

When Dr. Allen was satisfied that the nests had been deserted for good, the nesting trees were cut down, and he examined the nest-holes. To his surprise, he found only tiny shell fragments — there was no other evidence of occupation. The young had disappeared completely. Because the nests had not been under constant observation, nobody could say for certain what had happened to the young.

They may have been removed by the parents, but this was thought unlikely. Predation by owls, raccoons, or opossums was a more likely explanation. Dr. Allen hypothesized that because the ivory-bills were so reduced in numbers, inbreeding may have made the young too weak to survive, and they fell victim to predators.

By the late 1930s, the last hope for the ivory-bill was in a forest in Louisiana, known as the Singer Tract. Its eighty thousand acres were then still relatively uncut. The National Audubon Society and other interested organizations struggled to keep this land intact, and, in 1943, the director of the Audubon Society interceded with the President of the United States, Franklin Roosevelt, asking him to intervene. Roosevelt did not, and extensive logging extinguished the remaining hope for the bird's survival. The last bird was seen in the Singer Tract in 1944.

In the Apalachicola Swamp in northern Florida the last bird was seen in 1952, although there was an unconfirmed sighting at Gulf Hammock in northwestern Florida in 1963. In the same year, there was a reported sighting in South Carolina, and in 1966, there were reports from Texas.

THE SITUATION TODAY

The annual status report in the October, 1975, issue of *The Auk* sums up the situation:

> In May, 1971, a pair of ivory-billed woodpeckers was purportedly seen somewhere in Louisiana. Photographs were produced of one of these birds, clearly of this species, well up in the trunks of two large trees. Some who saw the photos were unable to confirm whether the subject was alive or was a museum mount. In spite of this, several less well-documented occurrences, and a host of rumors, there is little ground for optimism that the ivory-bill still exists. Presumed sightings of this species are greeted with such ferocious cross-examination by skeptics that those who have made valid sightings may well be cowed into silence by the prospects of inevitable inquest, in which their reputations may appear to be at stake. No holy grail has been more sought after on this continent, or aroused more rumors or recriminations.

In Cuba, the subspecies, the Cuban ivory-billed woodpecker (*Campephilus bairdii*), is almost gone as well and for much the same reason. And if any ivory-bills are left, which in itself is unlikely, there is little reason to suppose that recovery is now possible.

Bachman's Warbler

(Vermivora bachmanii)

Perhaps the happiest and most rewarding relationship between two naturalists was that between John James Audubon
(1785-1851) and the Reverend John Bachman (1790-1874) —
Audubon, the restless, imaginative, and talented traveler,
always seeking new species in a continent where such tower-
ing naturalists as Alexander Wilson, William Swainson, and
Spencer F. Baird were making new discoveries; Bachman, the
retiring German-Swiss. When still a young man, Bachman
moved to Charleston, South Carolina from New York State
because of ill health. In Charleston, he started a ministry at St.
John's Lutheran Church which was to last for sixty years.
Bachman's first love and duty were to his family and to his
parish; close behind in second place was his love of natural
history.

The relationship between the two men began in the autumn
of 1831, when Audubon's work was already widely recognized
following publication in Edinburgh of the first volume of his
Ornithological Biography. In order to study and paint, he jour-
neyed from New York to Florida by boat. He stopped in
Charleston, where he was invited to stay at Bachman's home.
He stayed for a month. After his departure, Bachman wrote to
Mrs. Audubon:

The last has been one of the happiest months of my life. I was an enthusiastic admirer of nature from my boyhood and fond of every branch of Natural History. Ornithology is, as a science, pursued by very few persons — and by none in this city. How gratifying it was, then, to become acquainted with a man who knew more about birds than any man now living — and who, at the same time, was communicative, intelligent, and amiable to an extent seldom found associated in the same individual. He has convinced me that I am but a novice in the study . . . he has taught me how much can be accomplished by a single individual, who will unite enthusiasm with industry. For the short month he remained with my family, we were inseparable. We were engaged in talking about Ornithology — in collecting birds — in seeing them prepared, and in laying plans for the accomplishment of that great work which he has undertaken. Time passed rapidly away, and it seems but as yesterday when we met, and now, alas! he is already separated from me — and in all human probability we shall never meet again. . . .

Here Bachman was wrong. From then on, they corresponded regularly on many subjects, and five years later Audubon and his son, John W., spent the winter in the Bachman household. John W. married Bachman's daughter in the spring of 1837, and in 1839, Victor Audubon, another son, married a second Bachman daughter. Their friendship and their work together (on the *Quadrupeds of North America*) continued until Audubon's death in 1851.

In the two years after Audubon's first visit, Bachman, the "novice in the study" discovered two new birds, both warblers, both near Charleston. First, in the spring of 1832, he discovered and collected a brown warbler with a rusty-colored cap, later to be named for William Swainson. Then, in July, 1833, he discovered another with an olive back, yellow face, and yellow underparts, dark cap, and large dark smear across its breast. Both birds were later described for science by Audubon, the second bird to be known henceforth as

Bachman's warbler — for his "amiable friend." Both, by a remarkable coincidence, were to disappear for the next fifty years. Swainson's has remained rare; Bachman's is the rarest song bird in North America — and probably was even then.

Since the last nest was found as long ago as 1920, we know little of this warbler's habits. We do know, however, that the only wintering area was in Cuba, where it fed on flowering hibiscus trees. In the spring and summer the small population was widely spread over the southeastern United States, and although nests were found in only five states (Missouri, Arkansas, Kentucky, Alabama, and South Carolina), it is likely that it bred in swamps over a larger area. Bachman's was an early migrant. It arrived in late February or early March in Florida and Louisiana and moved up the Mississippi valley (some moved eastward to South Carolina). We know it arrived on its breeding ground by mid-March, for nests have been found before the end of the month. The nest was built in bushes or vines from two to five feet above the ground. Three to four eggs were laid, but not much is known of nesting habits.

The Bachman's song is spirited and wiry, with a ventriloquial quality, delivered every six seconds. It seems to come from several directions at once, for the bird turns its head constantly while singing. It does most of its feeding in dense foliage high in the trees, consequently it was always hard to find. Naturalist Alexander Sprunt, Jr. commented: "I have spent as much as from two to three hours in swampy woods with a male singing ten times a minute at very close range and failed to get a glimpse of it."

THE DECLINE

In the latter part of the nineteenth century women's fashions demanded feathers, particularly for hats. Whole stuffed birds, or better (or worse) still, several might decorate one hat. No protection existed and no law prohibited using feathers from wild birds. There were hunters who made a career of shooting and trapping wild birds. One such hunter was Charles S. Galbraith. He operated near Mandeville, Louisiana, on the north shore of Lake Pontchartrain, about thirty miles from New Orleans. In the spring of 1886, he shot one Bachman's warbler, the next year six, the next year thirty-one. Today, one of these birds (without legs and mounted in an awkward pose for use on a hat), is in the American Museum of Natural History. In 1888, Galbraith, curious about his "new" bird, submitted it for identification — more than fifty years after Bachman first identified it!

Bachman's warblers must have been relatively numerous then because, on March 3, 1889, twenty-one perished striking a lighthouse in the Florida Keys, and, in 1892, Arthur T. Wayne collected fifty specimens on the Suwanee River in Florida.

TmShortt.

The first nest was discovered in Missouri in 1897, another in Kentucky in 1906, eight in South Carolina in 1906 and 1907, and one more in Alabama in 1920. Bachman's has been seen in states as far north as Virginia during the nesting season, but no nests have been discovered. Why? The reason can be found in Wayne's description of the bird's typical nesting habitat: " ... I always keep out of such places after April 10 on account of the myriads of ticks and red bugs which infest them. Then, too, such places are simply impenetrable on account of the dense blackberry vines, matted with grape vines, fallen logs piled one upon another, and a dense growth of low bushes." Otto Widmann, discoverer of the first nest (in 1897) said the nesting area "extended over two acres of blackberry brambles among a medley of half-decayed and lately felled tree tops, lying in pools of water, everything dripping wet with dew in the forenoon, and steaming under a broiling sun in the afternoon."

In the last fifty years, few Bachman's warblers have been seen. Each year between 1948 and 1953, some were sighted in the same swamp where they were discovered in 1833, but no nest was found. In 1975, the American Ornithologists' Union reported:

> This rarest and least known of North American warblers appears to be continuing its decline towards extinction. The only recent sighting in the Gulf States is one off the coast of Louisiana in 1973. On Francis Marion National Forest and adjacent plantation swamplands in South Carolina, sporadic sightings continue to be made, the most recent being a male in April, 1975. In fact, no female has been seen for several years, nor has a nest been found.

It seems likely that the Bachman's warbler was on its way out even before plume traders, scientific collectors, and lighthouses got at this small population. Skimpy evidence points to an increase in numbers between 1890 and 1900, and a rapid decline thereafter, but it could be that no one noticed them before Mr. Galbraith took his thirty-eight birds.

Kirtland's Warbler

(Dendroica kirtlandii)

The Kirtland's warbler breeds on the ground under jack pines of a certain age in the northern part of the lower peninsula of Michigan — and nowhere else. Of the fifty or so North American warbler species, its nesting requirements are the most specific. Every nest ever found has been within a radius of sixty miles of the spot where the first nest was found in 1903.

Today, the Kirtland's warbler population has shrunk to under four hundred — its ability to survive is doubtful.

The song is low pitched (for a warbler), with a series of rapid notes followed by others in a higher pitch. The whole song lasts about two seconds and is repeated from six to ten times a minute. The bird is about five inches long, yellow below and bluish-gray above, with two indistinct white wing bars and a white eye ring. The back is clearly marked with black streaks. The female is similar to the male, but duller in color.

HISTORY

In 1852, Spencer F. Baird of the Smithsonian Institution identified Kirtland's as a new species. He also named it. Baird had been attending a meeting in Cincinnati, and, before returning to Washington, stopped in Cleveland to visit his friend, Dr.

Jared P. Kirtland. Kirtland, a talented naturalist, teacher, and doctor, gave Baird a specimen of an unknown warbler, which he, in turn, had received from his collector son-in-law, Charles Pease.

Dr. Kirtland's specimen, however, was not the first. In October, 1841, Samuel Cabot, a New England sea captain, took one on his ship then on passage between the Bahamian island of Abaco and Cuba. After a long stay in Yucatan Cabot returned to Boston, and forgot all about the bird. It collected dust in a drawer until 1865, when it came to light. This particular bird was undoubtedly on migration to its only winter home — the Bahamas. In 1879, bird watcher Charles B. Cory found the Kirtland's wintering on Andros. Since then, the bird has been seen on several of the Bahamian islands. In 1879, it was described as "not uncommon" there. Recent attempts, however, to find wintering birds have been unsuccessful. Obviously, it was more common then than it is today; why, will soon become apparent.

Not until 1903 was the breeding ground discovered — by accident. E.H. Frothingham, a zoologist from the University of Michigan Museum, and his friend T.G. Gale were trout fishing on the Au Sable River when they heard a bird song which neither recognized. Gale shot one bird for identification purposes. Norman A. Wood of the University of Michigan identified the specimen as a Kirtland's warbler. More importantly, he realized from the date of the sighting (June 13) that the bird was probably nesting. He set out at once to investigate.

He journeyed first by train, then two days by row boat. Finally he reached the part of Oscoda County where his friends had shot the bird, and between July 2 and July 7 he heard and saw five singing males and one female, but could find no nest. He moved several miles to the west to an area which had burned some years before. It now supported a growth of jack pine three to ten feet high. From the notes made as he searched, one can sense his excitement:

I have just found a pair of Kirtland's Warblers and, as I write, the female is three feet away, fluttering her wings, and seems very anxious. I am near a small heap of brush and logs and maybe the nest is here.... As I go around on my hands and knees, I see she keeps very near.... The male is on top of a dead stub twenty feet high.... Near the top of the stub is a small hole, it may be the nest is there, although I have not seen the female go there.... Down the jack pine he went.... No bird, no nest! I watched a few minutes longer and saw the female in the low jack pines. I watched her and she seemed very uneasy (having just been flushed from the nest). I began looking carefully on the ground, as I had made up my mind it would be found there. Suddenly I saw the nest!.... In the nest were two young birds a few days old and, as luck would have it, one beautiful egg.... Pinkish white, thinly sprinkled with chocolate brown spots gathered in a wreath at the larger end.

After Wood's discovery, researchers spent years ferreting out the bird's secrets: Why are its nesting requirements so specific? Why does it nest only under jack pines of a certain age? Why only in this part of Michigan, when jack pines grow from the Northwest Territories to Nova Scotia, and south to the end of Lake Michigan? Why are there so few birds?

In 1930, Josselyn Van Tyne, curator of birds at the University of Michigan Museum of Zoology, set out to find the answers. During twenty-two of the twenty-six years between 1930 and 1956, he spent part of each summer in the nesting area, and five weeks in the winter in the Bahamas on its wintering ground. Early in 1957 he died, without publishing his findings. Van Tyne's records, written on a series of file cards, were subsequently used by Harold Mayfield, who, in 1944, had joined Van Tyne in his studies. Mayfield's book, *The Kirtland's Warbler*, published in 1960, is a classic of painstaking research; in it many of the Kirtland's secrets are exposed.

LIFE CYCLE

Michigan's pine forests grow in an area of loose sand, with an inch or less thick cover of humus. Historically, there has been much burning of the more mature trees from both natural and unnatural causes.

Kirtland's warblers first nest in a burned area six to thirteen years after a fire, when the jack pines are about six feet high; they cease to use the area when the pines grow to more than fifteen feet high. Thus, fire is essential for creating and recreating suitable habitat. Since most fires start late in the summer when the forest is at its driest, the birds are not adversely affected — warblers are present in the area only during its period of growth, when a heavy groundcover of blueberries and other shrubs emerges. The groundcover disappears as the trees grow, expanding to shade the ground. The tree's lower branches die also. How long the Kirtland's uses a burned area, depends on the quality of the soil and the rate of the vegetation's growth — it can be anywhere from six to nineteen years, but twelve is average.

Females choose the nest site and build the nest. They need living lower branches to hide them while moving from nest to tree — at least, that is the theory.

Kirtland's warblers prefer to live in loose colonies — not that they associate with one another other than by song, but it is unusual to find one nest out of sound of another.

About mid-May, males start to arrive on the nesting grounds, a few days earlier than the females. Immediately, the male bird begins to establish his territory. He defends it tenaciously until the young are fledged. In size, territories range anywhere from 1.5 to 16.5 acres; most males, however, appear to defend an area of eight to ten acres. Normally nests are at least two hundred yards apart, occasionally closer.

To digress slightly, it now becomes obvious that a "colony" must have an adequate area of suitable contiguous habitat, a habitat where all the trees are approximately the same size. It has been found that areas smaller than eighty acres do not attract the Kirtland's. In earlier times, when fires were started only by lightning and burned uncontrolled, very large patches emerged. Today, fires can be controlled quickly. Consequently, there are no large burned units.

What makes this part of Michigan unique? And is it indeed unique? The answer is yes. Elsewhere, jack pines grow and burn, leaving adequate openings, but with the new trees growing in clusters. Clusters are not suitable for the Kirtland's: groundcover is slower to grow and the usefulness of planted trees is shorter. Farther north in Canada, jack pines grow on moister ground where the soil is not as porous. In Michigan, however, the light sand permits rain to seep away quickly, leaving almost no standing water — a requisite for a ground-nesting bird. During the glacial periods, jack pine stands extended much farther south, and probably the Kirtland's nested over a wider area; today, it breeds almost on the southern limit of the pine barrens.

Breeding habits are similar to those of other warblers. When the female arrives, she joins the male and for about two weeks they are together on the territory, defending it against their own kind. The female makes the nest on the ground. It is seldom more than three feet away from the base of a pine and always under a canopy of groundcover, either dead grass or a low bush. The male is in attendance, singing constantly; not just for the joy of it, but to maintain the territory against intruders. Nest finding would be a matter of pure luck without the male's singing.

After two days work, the nest is essentially complete, but two more days are spent fussing with the lining — perhaps to keep the female busy while waiting for the first egg. She lays her eggs (usually five) consecutively each morning. Incubation begins on the day before the last egg is laid. It lasts thirteen to fourteen days. The male feeds her during this period, and, although she leaves the nest from time to time, she is on it for ninety percent of the time during daylight hours as well as all night.

Most birds hatch from June 12 to June 26. Hatchlings first leave the nest on their ninth or tenth day. They are already capable of short flight, but rely on their parents for food. At this time the male and female divide their young, and, although the whole family remains in the nest territory for some time and their paths may cross from time to time, in essence, they go their separate ways. Gradually they move farther and farther away from the nest, and, by about the beginning of August, the young have parted company from their parents for good.

THE DECLINE

The Kirtland's deadly enemy is the brown-headed cowbird. Cowbirds (*Molothrus ater*) do not build their own nests, but lay their eggs in warbler, vireo, and sparrow nests. Some species have developed defences against the cowbird: for example, building a new layer on the old nest and laying again, or moving away, or somehow getting rid of the unwanted egg or eggs.

Unfortunately, the Kirtland's warbler has not learned to defend itself. Invariably it raises the cowbird nestling as its own.

How does this happen? Covertly, the female cowbird watches the Kirtland's building her nest; and lays her eggs in it either before or at the same time as her hapless hostess. Cowbird eggs hatch in twelve days; the cowbird chick weighs six times more than the warbler chick. To add insult to injury, female cowbirds frequently remove all or some of the warbler eggs, then lay up to four of their own. Before the cowbird-control program began, more than half of the Kirtland's nests were found to contain one or more cowbird eggs, and, when more than one cowbird chick is hatched, the chances of any warblers surviving are zero. If ony one cowbird is hatched, at least some warblers survive. In parasited nests, on an average, warblers produce 1.4 young of their own; in unparasited, 2.2.

The cowbird was originally a bird of the plains and until about 1850, was virtually unknown in the east. Clearing the land to field and pasture, where cattle replaced the buffalo, created ideal cowbird habitat. Consequently, before 1850, the Kirtland's nesting success rate was probably much higher and the population larger — at least so it is assumed.

The warbler range was first settled by man in 1854, but not until 1875, when the railways went through, did lumbering become important. From then until 1900, virtually all the red and white pine was cut, leaving only the worthless jack pine. The slash was left on the ground, and from mid-summer on huge fires raged — creating large areas of suitable habitat. There was even intentional burning to encourage blueberry bushes. And, as the cowbird was not yet a major factor, the warbler population increased.

Since early lumbering days, attitudes toward uncontrolled fires have changed. Wildfires are now suppressed as soon as is humanly possible. And very few areas burn long enough to create suitable future habitat.

We have already mentioned that in the Bahamas during the 1880s, the Kirtland's was "not uncommon"; now it is seldom seen there, despite an increase in the number of interested observers. This fact alone supports the theory that the species was then more numerous. Since 1879, some seventy-one specimens have been collected on the wintering ground. Of these, forty-four were taken between 1880 and 1889.

RECOVERY EFFORTS

In 1961, the United States Forest Service established the 4,010-acre Kirtland's Warbler Management Area. Realizing the Kirtland's need for larger burned areas, a plan calling for controlled burning was brought into being: twelve 320-acre sectors were set aside, each to be burned in rotation.

First, they cut all trees, except for a few per acre for seeds. (Jack pine cones open only when hot; when hot, they spread their seeds widely.) May, 1964, was the date of the first burn, called Operation Popcone, and by that September two hundred seedlings per acre had germinated. The Forest Service, encouraged by this initial success, masterminded a sixty-year cycle: one of the twelve sectors is to be burned approximately every five years.

POPULATION FLUCTUATIONS (1951-1974)

Until 1951, when the first census was organized, nobody really understood the Kirtland's plight. In that census, thirty-two expert observers covering ninety-one-mile-square sectors, counted 432 singing males; an indication that the whole population was under a thousand. The 1961 census counted 502 males. Unfortunately, in the 1960s, the cowbird population was also on the increase, and the 1971 census (taken by forty-eight observers) tallied only 201 singing males — a decrease of sixty percent.

Harold Mayfield reported: "The bird has collapsed down into the center of its entire historical breeding range, leaving the periphery virtually empty."

In 1971, warblers nested only in twenty-seven-square-mile sections; in 1951 they nested in ninety-one-square-mile sections. Here was a serious setback. What had caused the decline between 1951 and 1971? Nobody knew for certain — cowbirds, heavy cutting of the pine forests in the Bahamas — these may have been contributing factors; there may have been others. Mayfield pressed for cowbird control, but little was done.

In the mid-sixties, there was some shooting and trapping of the cowbird, and even with these limited control measures, Kirtland's nesting success improved. In the control areas, the level of cowbird parasitism dropped from eighty-six percent of the nests to twenty-one percent.

In 1972, the trapping program was stepped up. Using fifteen large wire traps baited with sunflower seeds and decoy cowbirds, twenty-two hundred cowbirds were caught. In 1973, eighteen traps caught 3,305 cowbirds. The success of this experiment soon became obvious: in a test area of Kirtland's nests, not one was parasited. Nests averaged 2.79 young — three times the success rate of cowbird-infested areas.

The 1973 census results showed both gains and losses: the nesting area had decreased to twenty-five-square-mile sections, but 215 singing males were counted — an increase of fourteen from the previous year. By June 3, 1974, twenty-two traps had caught more than three thousand cowbirds, with little evidence of their eggs reported.

In 1974, the census was held as usual in June. The result: only 167 singing males — a decrease of twenty-three percent in one year. Why? Nobody knows.

Back in the fifties, Mayfield believed that without cowbird control, the Kirtland's warbler was doomed. It now appears doomed anyway — despite the mighty efforts made on its behalf.

Ipswich Sparrow

(Passerculus sandwichensis princeps)

During the Pleistocene period when the seas subsided, vast areas of sand emerged off what is now the east coast of North America. These high dunes were unstable, and prevailing westerly winds gradually reduced them until now the only remnant is Sable Island. It is a narrow crescent of sand, ninety miles south of the east end of Nova Scotia, twenty-two miles long, and nowhere more than three-quarters of a mile wide. It lies along the direction of the prevailing wind — from southwest to northeast.

Since its discovery 450 years ago, Sable Island has become famous as the graveyard of the Atlantic. Many ships have perished on its foggy shores. Dire predictions have been made that it is fast disappearing: wind and water erosion at the west end is more rapid than the compensating build-up of dunes at the east end. Only half the island is verdant, the rest is bare sand. The verdant dunes are stable and reach a height of about eighty feet. The principal cover is marram, a coarse spiky grass which grows in clumps to about a foot high, either in pure stands or mixed with beach pea. There are some areas of peaty soil where shrubs grow — blueberry, rose, mayberry, winterberry, juniper, and crowberry. There are no trees.

Man populated the island with cattle, sheep, horses, rabbits, foxes, and cats. Cattle, sheep, rabbits, and foxes were removed many years ago. Only the horses, a few domestic cats, and the personnel of the meteorological station and lighthouses remain.

Much damage has been done to the fragile vegetation, which depends on the stability of the dunes. Animals' hooves and intensive grazing have reduced the vegetated cover.

Twenty years ago a narrow strip of brackish water, Wallace Lake, stretched for nine miles along the island's interior, protected on both sides by high dunes. Today, the dunes on the south side have blown away. The lake is now three ponds, and most of it has been filled in.

Sable Island is the only nesting ground of the Ipswich sparrow, a large, pale race of the Savannah sparrow (*Passerculus sandwichensis*). It is about five and a half inches long, pale, almost white below, with gray streaking on the breast.

The upper parts are grayer and paler than on other sparrows. In summer there is a yellow patch above the eye, but in winter it disappears in most individuals.

Until 1973 the Ipswich sparrow rejoiced as a full species (*Passerculus princeps*), although authorities had long believed it to be a subspecies of the Savannah. That year the American Ornithologists' Union re-designated it as a subspecies — an interesting change because it recognized that the Ipswich has not been in breeding isolation long enough to make it incapable of breeding with mainland Savannahs.

In their original and intensive studies of the Ipswich, W.T. Stobo and Ian McLaren, biologists from Dalhousie University in Halifax, were the first to discover female Ipswich sparrows breeding on mainland Nova Scotia, paired with male Savannahs. No case has yet been observed of two Ipswich sparrows breeding anywhere except on Sable Island, nor is there a known case of a male Ipswich paired with a female Savannah. For our purposes, it is enough to quote from Stobo and McLaren's book *The Ipswich Sparrow*.

> The Ipswich sparrows form an adaptively unique population with its own evolutionary tendencies. The limited hybridization between it and the mainland Savannah sparrow is no greater than that occurring between other populations that are generally accepted as species and probably has no population consequences.

And they summarize their position:

> The American Ornithologists' Union's 1973 decision should be understood to be a subjective one about the importance of genetic differences involved in this and comparable groups of birds. Certainly the Ipswich sparrow must be viewed as an exceptionally well-differentiated subspecies by prevailing standards.

Stobo and McLaren's disagreement with the decision, while not stated, is apparent.

HISTORY

The residents of Sable Island had long known a sparrow which they called "the gray bird," but not until December 4, 1868, when the ornithologist C.J. Maynard shot an unknown member of the family near Ipswich, Massachusetts, was it described. He first mistook it for a Baird's sparrow (*Ammodramus bairdii*), a wanderer from the western plains, but later realized he had collected a bird of a new species. A set of eggs at the National Museum in Washington, which had been collected on Sable Island in 1862 and labelled "Savannah Sparrow," was found to be larger than others of this species. In 1892, a specimen bird was collected on Sable Island, compared with Maynard's, and found to be the same species. Thus the breeding ground was established. In 1895, Jonathan Dwight visited Sable Island to study the bird's nesting behavior; in 1902, W.E. Saunders arrived for the same reason. Nothing more was done until 1948, when John Jackson Elliott made a study which appeared in 1968 in Bent's *Life Histories*. And between 1968 and 1974 Stobo and McLaren carried out their minutely detailed research. Their monograph was published in 1975; they had "found out a great deal more about the Ipswich sparrow than is known about most birds."

THE SITUATION TODAY

Scientific research on any animal or bird species can be frustrating in that the researcher can deal only with fact, limiting his interpretation to what can be deduced. The amateur is tempted to jump to convenient conclusions.

Until fifty years ago, the Ipswich sparrow was the only land bird to nest on this remote sandbar (it has since been joined by the house sparrow (*Passer domesticus*), a few brown-headed cowbirds (*Molothrus ater*), and crows (*Corvus brachyrhynchos*). Has it been there since the Pleistocene sand emergence, of which Sable Island is a tiny remnant? Or did it appear later, to

TM Shortt.

develop its own characteristics and preferences? Were there other endemic species which have since disappeared? Although the American Ornithologists' Union is probably correct in designating it a subspecies of the Savannah sparrow, its niche is unique. Adaptability to its sand-grass environment has increased its special requirements and maintained its stability.

The spring population on Sable Island varies between two thousand and three thousand birds. The autumn population can be as many as fifteen thousand.

Every year all but a few migrate northward to Nova Scotia, then drift southward along the eastern seaboard. The main winter concentrations are between Virginia and New Jersey, although a few reach Florida and a few stay in Nova Scotia; but all remain within a few hundred yards of the ocean dunes. Every year about seventy-five percent die during the winter; those that survive return to Sable Island.

Each year in late December bird counts are made all over North America by thousands of people, each group being responsible for a pre-determined area. Stobo and McLaren, using information from these Christmas counts made on the eastern seaboard between 1937 and 1972, have been unable to detect any long-term trends in the population, despite substantial short-term variations; it may be that the numbers today are not much different from a hundred years ago.

LIFE CYCLE

During the winter Ipswich sparrows feed and rest on coastal dunes. Residential and recreational development and commercial excavation of dune sand have reduced their available winter habitat, and this is the principal threat to the bird's survival. By the end of the winter, dunes provide little food for the Ipswich and other migrating birds; the dunes are wind-blown and sterile.

Northerly movement is under way by mid-March and continues for about a month. Some birds enter Nova Scotia at its southwestern tip, others cross the Bay of Fundy, then take an overland route until they reach their take-off point to Sable Island. By whatever route, birds arrive in April, and by the end of the month they are all on Sable Island. Weather is important during this period — the main migration occurs when winds are in the west or northwest and average ten miles an hour. Despite their early arrival, weather on Sable Island in May is not conducive to nesting. (The mean temperature is about 7.5°C, compared to a more compatible 11.5°C in June.)

Nests are on the ground in a hollow scratched into the surface, and usually under the cover of a shrub. Three to six eggs are laid, with an average of four. The first clutch is usually complete by the end of May (about ten days later in cold wet years). Incubation averages ten days, and the young remain in the nest for a further ten to twelve days. The young leave the nest several days before they can fly. During this period they are fed by both parents.

The female, however, is already making a second nest and courting — the period between departure of the young and laying the second clutch is only a few days. Winter die-off being high, obviously a high reproductive rate is vital. Nesting success averages a high eighty-five percent of eggs hatched, and in good years females average three nests: a total of nearly twelve young fledged and alive in autumn. Even four successful nests are not uncommon between June and mid-September.

Today, predation is minimal on Sable Island, although gulls and crows do take a few young. Heavy rain and a cold June have a more serious impact on the survival of young birds. By the end of each summer, the population has grown severalfold, numbers depending on how many survived the winter, and the summer's weather. Between 1967 and 1974, the lowest spring population was 2,100 in 1970, following a wet summer in 1969 (when the autumn population was only 7,500 birds). The increase in the summer of 1970 was nearly six-fold — 12,200 birds. The highest autumn count was 14,750 in 1973.

In October, all but a few birds leave the island.

THE FUTURE

Despite the restricted size of its breeding habitat on Sable Island, the Ipswich sparrow population has room to expand. The limit to growth is the availability of winter feeding in the only habitat the Ipswich sparrow will use — open beach dunes. The Ipswich's relatively short tail restricts its man-euverability, and limits it to open country. (The smaller, but relatively longer-tailed associated species, the Savannah spar-row, is better adapted to flying in close surroundings.)

Beach dunes from New Jersey to Virginia must be preserved if the sparrow is to survive. Fortunately, preservation of beach dunes ties in with the demand for human recreation. The bird's summer habitat is more controllable, at least in the short term. Oil exploration on the Grand Banks and around Sable Island could be devastating to the vegetation and dunes of this fragile sandbar, but it has been found that wheeled traffic has little impact if restricted to bare sand. About half the Island's vegetated cover has disappeared as a result of human and animal interference, but much of it can be restored. With adequate vegetation to inhibit wind erosion, there is less reason to fear that the island will eventually disappear.

Doctors Stobo and McLaren, who know more about the Ipswich sparrow than anyone else, consider that although it "is in no immediate danger of extinction, its longer-term survival is clearly in the hands of man." Their conclusion would indicate that this bird has no place on the Endangered Species list, but until the winter habitat is made more secure, it remains potentially vulnerable.

Dusky Seaside Sparrow

(*Ammospiza nigrescens*)

The song begins with two or three faint notes, followed by a stronger, higher-pitched buzz, the whole lasting about two seconds. Only the male sings, and only while nesting or defending his territory. In the early morning during the nesting season, he sings his song as often as every six or seven seconds, less often during the day, more frequently again at dusk.

Seaside sparrows occur in nine distinct forms, ranging from Massachusetts to Texas. Maritime in their nesting and feeding habits, they are found only in salt grasses. They differ somewhat from one another but all are grayer and darker than other sparrows (particularly on the head and back), have relatively long bills, a yellow patch before the eye, and a short, narrow tail.

Only the dusky and the Smyrna seaside sparrows are in danger of extinction.

LIFE CYCLE

The first seaside sparrow was identified as a new species in 1810 by Alexander Wilson, the early ornithologist, on the New Jersey coast near the present Ocean City. His observations, written in 1811 (as recorded in A.C. Bent's *Life History*) are worth quoting:

> It inhabits the low rush-covered sea islands of our Atlantic coast, where I first found it; keeping almost continually within the boundaries of tidewater, except when long and violent east or northeasterly storms, with high tides, compel it to seek the shore. On these occasions, it courses along the margin and among the holes and interstices of the weeds and sea-wrack, with a rapidity equalled only by the nimblest of our sandpipers, and very much in their manner.

Each race of seaside sparrow has its specific breeding range along the Atlantic and Gulf coasts. Most tend to be non-migratory, but some do move south in the winter. For example, the northern seaside sparrow (*Ammospiza maritima maritima*) breeds from Massachusetts to northern North Carolina, and winters south to Florida. MacGillivray's seaside sparrow (*Ammospiza maritima macgillivraii*) breeds from North Carolina to southern Georgia. The other subspecies range from around the Florida and Gulf coasts to Texas.

The dusky's story is different. It probably has the most limited range of any North American bird — a tiny area within a ten-mile radius of Titusville, Breward County, on the east coast of central Florida. On this patch, the dusky sparrow's small population remained relatively stable for thousands of years. When it was discovered by Charles J. Maynard on March 17, 1872, the bird was quite common. DDT-spraying between 1942 and 1953 caused it great harm. Because the dusky is non-migratory and its limited habitat has been so seriously disturbed, today its chances of survival are slim.

SPECIES OR SUBSPECIES?

The dusky's range is bounded on the north by extensive growths of black mangrove. The mangrove effectively separates the dusky from its nearest seaside sparrow neighbor, the Smyrna seaside sparrow, *Ammospiza maritima pelonota*. In 1949,

George Sutton, the prominent artist and ornithologist, noted that the two were separated by about thirty miles; a distance which has since grown to seventy-five miles. The nearest population to the west is on Florida's other coast, some 125 miles

away. Cape Sable sparrows, also endangered (which some consider a race of the seaside family), are 250 miles to the southwest. Separate and isolated, the dusky's ability to reproduce with other seaside sparrows will probably never be put to the test under natural conditions.

THE DECLINE

Before the DDT era, no real concern was felt about the dusky's future. The salt grasses, on which the birds relied for nesting, grew close to the tide limits where they fed. Forty-five years ago, bird watcher Donald J. Nicholson writes how prevalent they were:

> Upon entering their habitat one sees individuals on all sides. They seem to appear from nowhere, perch a few moments on the tops of the vegetation, and scold continuously. Here and there males chase the females in zigzag courses, flying low and very swiftly just above the grass tops, sometimes for several hundred yards or more. Others

from many directions simultaneously sing their rasping, far-carrying songs from prominent perches atop grass or rush stems. Here and there an exuberant male performs his courtship song flight. Bubbling over with his jerky, rasping, erratic song he flutters slowly almost straight upward to a height of twenty or thirty feet, pauses a moment at the apex, and then, still singing, descends just as slowly to perch in the grass tops again.

Today one seldom hears the "rasping, far-carrying songs," or sees "an exuberant male." What happened? To answer this question, we must first understand the area. Titusville, the center of the breeding range, is on Highway 1, which runs the length of the Florida east coast. About five miles to the west, is the St. Johns River, and to the east, the Indian River. Both run almost straight north-south. Farther to the east, beyond the Indian River, is a string of low-lying peninsulas and islands. Cape Kennedy, formerly Cape Canaveral, is at the tip. The dusky's breeding grounds are along the St. Johns River; somewhat inland on the east side of the Indian River on marshes which face the west; and on Merritt Island which is to the south, but still on the Indian River.

The space center on Cape Kennedy stopped residential development in the area, but, in 1956, a program of impounding the marshes on the east side of the Indian River began, in order to exclude the salt water and thus maintain a level of fresh water deep enough to reduce mosquitoes. The result? Salt hay, bunch grass, and black rush, in which the duskies nest, has now been replaced with freshwater plants, particularly cattails, not suitable for nesting. The remaining suitable nesting habitat is usually too far from the feeding area. Forty years ago, Nicholson found nests as close together as forty feet. Today, as the salt grasses thin, nests are farther and farther apart. Added to this, water from the St. Johns farther upstream has been diverted, thus lowering the water table. Duskies prefer damp but unflooded marsh, strongly salty. Such marshes are harder and harder to find in the Titusville area.

Dusky seaside sparrow ▶

(The nest is made in dense clusters of grass a few inches above the high water level.)

Impoundment of the salt marshes, rendering them fresh, has introduced at least two new predators. The dusky in its prime was able to tolerate traditional predation from rice rats, four species of snakes, ants, and raccoons. Freshwater predators, however, it cannot tolerate. The fresh water has brought pig frogs, which take dusky nestlings, as do boat-tailed grackles which now nest in the bushes which have grown up on the dikes.

Some years ago, the St. Johns National Wildlife Refuge was created to the west. This area has been adversely affected by drainage, pastures, highways, and housing developments. In 1968, 894 male duskies were counted here; in 1972, 110, and in 1973, 54. Two earlier fires were probably responsible for this dramatic decline, while another fire in the winter of 1975 burned out most of the suitable habitat in the St. Johns area. The latest count? Fewer than one dozen males in the spring of 1976.

In the Merritt Island National Wildlife Refuge to the east, the dusky has virtually disappeared. Dr. James L. Baker, a wildlife biologist with the United States Fish and Wildlife Service, who heads the recovery team at Merritt Island, says there are now fewer than one hundred pairs in existence.

THE FUTURE

Organized recovery efforts by the Fish and Wildlife Service of the Department of the Interior are just beginning . Plans do include, however, renovation of previously impounded areas in order to revert them back to high salt marshes, and in the Merritt Island Refuge, it will be necessary to introduce birds from the St. Johns Refuge, provided there are enough left to transplant.

Despite these efforts, the dusky's future is still doubtful. Numbers have declined to such a critical level that they may disappear entirely before the habitat can be restored.

Cape Sable Sparrow

(*Ammospiza maritima mirabilis*)

The Cape Sable sparrow was the last North American bird to be identified as a separate species. Discovered in 1918 by Florida bird specialist Arthur H. Howell in Cape Sable, Florida, it had been overlooked by the early ornithologists because it was so like the swamp, savannah, and grasshopper sparrows, which share the Cape Sable's range in winter. In addition, its numbers were few, and it lived only in inaccessible, swampy prairie.

Since the Cape Sable's discovery, it has been the center of some mild controversy in academic circles. Is it a species or a subspecies? Howell called it the Cape Sable *seaside* sparrow, believing it to be a race of the seaside family. The American Ornithologists' Union thought not, and, by 1957, had elevated the Cape Sable to the rank of a full species. Other voices from academe disagreed — claiming the breeding isolation of the Cape Sable was of fairly recent geological occurrence, and that it *could* perhaps breed with seasides. As the closest seaside sparrow population is one hundred and fifty miles away, and, as the Cape Sable is non-migratory, there is little chance of this hypothesis ever being tested.

Whatever its true and proper rank, the Cape Sable sparrow does look different: it has a greener tinge than seaside sparrows; the underparts are whiter with distinct, greenish stripes. The spot in front of the eye is yellow; the seaside sparrow's spot is white. These differences sound recognizable on paper, but even those who know the bird well will not hazard to make an identification in the field, particularly during the winter when the Cape Sable shares its range with the similar swamp, savannah, and grasshopper sparrows. Many wrong identifications have been made, perhaps the most glaring in the immediate vicinity of Cape Sable, where the bird was first discovered and from where it was extirpated by a fierce hurricane in 1935. Here, between 1935 and 1970, it was reported regularly. One reliable report of six adults with five juveniles in 1970 raised hopes that it would re-establish on the Cape, but Harold W. Werner, who specializes in the study of the bird and who made the report, has since advised that it appears to be doing poorly.

It is only in the spring and summer nesting season, when the Cape Sable is singing, and when other sparrows are breeding elsewhere, that it is safe to make a sight identification.

HABITAT

Where is its range? From Cape Sable, the southernmost point on Florida's mainland, to Everglades City, some miles to the northwest. Here live the world's few remaining Cape Sable sparrows. To find out why only a few remain, let us first look at the bird's habitat, starting at Cape Sable.

Cape Sable has a sand and gravel shore, with unprotected marshes extending inland behind it. From the Cape northward, most of the coastline consists of mangroves extending from two to fifteen miles inland. The mangroves are interlaced with creeks and bays, some navigable by small boats. Here and there are salt marshes. Farther east, beyond the mangroves, lies a strip of relatively open marshes where the water ranges from salt to fresh. Still farther east is a mixture of cypress swamps, pine woods, and wet, freshwater prairie (which tends to dry out during periods of drought). This freshwater area is fed by the Everglades, a "river" some thirty

miles wide. The Everglades, with its almost imperceptible movement through the sawgrass and swamps, drains Lake Okeechobee. But it is in the intermediate zone, in the wet freshwater prairie between the mangroves and the Everglades, that the Cape Sable sparrow still lives on. Why is it in trouble?

The answer lies in its habitat. Any sedentary bird, with a range (for the whole population) extending over only a few miles, is exposed to calamity — natural and man-made. And the west coast of Florida gets more than its share — hurricanes, droughts, fires, developers, and, to a lesser extent, predators.

When hurricanes strike this low-lying coast, the damage can be devastating. Winds of a hundred miles an hour and more can drive before them a wall of water eight feet high. If they strike at night, so much the worse; the birds are asleep and have no chance. The mangrove belt to the north shields the inland marshes somewhat, but the marshes on Cape Sable have no protective shield.

On September 1, 1935, there was a particularly violent storm, and it struck at night. Vast amounts of water poured over the Cape Sable beaches, instantly filling the marshes, causing havoc and destruction to all wildlife. If a storm breaks in daylight, birds have a chance — they can move to higher ground. Hurricane Donna (September, 1960), for example, struck Cape Sable at daybreak and in the course of the morning moved up the coast to Everglades City. But it did no great harm to the Cape Sable sparrows, for, despite high winds and flooding, birds were seen nesting there the next spring.

Fires can be even more catastrophic particularly after a drought. In May, 1962, two major fires broke out, eventually joined, and destroyed a total 185,000 acres. Much of the Cape Sable's most favored habitat was destroyed. In the burned-out area they disappeared completely; in the unburned area, some sparrows survived.

Drought parches the marshes destroying insects on which the sparrow feeds. (Unlike most of its family, the Cape Sable sparrow is only a marginal eater of seeds.)

Mangroves are another threat. Their constant encroachment reduces the sparrow's habitat. In inland Florida, intensive farming has increased the volume of silt in the rivers and the Everglades. Eventually, silt covers the natural sandy beds in which the marsh grasses grow, provides growing areas where mangrove seeds can germinate, and mangroves spread farther inland. To illustrate how prevalent they have become, one can travel for miles in a small boat through the estuary streams under an unbroken canopy of tall mangroves.

In drier areas, brush and exotic trees are invading the grassy marshes, but recent experiments in the controlled use of fire have had encouraging results. In 1972, for example, a small portion of an area called Taylor Slough was fire-cleared of brush — in the following spring, Cape Sables nested there.

THE SITUATION TODAY

The Cape Sable sparrow has almost disappeared from much of its original range. Surveys made between 1952 and 1955 indicated a fair population in the Ochopee area. Since then the area has been plagued by development, drought, and fire — in 1970, only ten singing males could be found; in 1972, five; in 1975, two.

On the credit side — in 1971, a large population of approximately one thousand was discovered in the Taylor Slough area, on land protected by the Everglades National Park. Here, the birds are scattered over some 32,000 acres and appear to be holding their own.

Under ideal conditions Cape Sables can produce as many as three broods of three to four young between February and August; the time span from incubation to independence is only forty-five days. Nesting ceases with the onset of heavy rains and marsh flooding (usually in September). The Taylor Slough area has only a three-month rainy period (other areas in the bird's range have a longer rainy period). Thus, the area is favorable for nesting. Favorable nesting conditions are vital, because this recently discovered group estimated to number well over a thousand, comprises almost the whole of the known population of the species.

WHAT IS BEING DONE?

So far, recovery efforts have concentrated on research of habitat requirements, restoration of habitat, and maintenance of habitat and water levels. The program is expensive: water levels of marshes must be manipulated; controlled fires must eliminate brush, exotic plants, and exotic trees; privately owned lands must be first bought, then restored to suitable habitat.

Bibliography

Aldrich, J.W., and Baer, K.P. "Status and Speciation in the Mexican Duck." *The Wilson Bulletin*, Vol. 82 No. 1, March 1970, pp. 63–73.

Allen, A.A., and Kellogg, P.P. "Recent Observations on the Ivory-billed Woodpecker." *The Auk*, Vol. 54 No. 2, April 1937, pp. 164–184.

Allen, R.P. Whooping Crane Report. Research Report No. 3, National Audubon Society, New York.

American Ornithologists' Union. Report of Committee on Conservation 1974–75. Supplement to *The Auk*, Vol. 92 No. 4, October 1975, and 1975–76, Vol. 93 No. 5, October 1976.

Baker, J.L. "Preliminary Studies of the Dusky Seaside Sparrow on the St. Johns National Wildlife Refuge." *Proceedings of the 27th Annual Conference of the Southeastern Association of Game and Fish Commissioners*, 1973, pp. 207–214.

Banko, W.E. The Trumpeter Swan, Its History, Habits, and Population in the United States. North American Fauna No. 63, U.S. Fish and Wildlife Service, 1960.

Bent, A.C. *Life Histories of North American Birds of Prey*. U.S. National Museum Bulletin, No. 167, 1937. The Smithsonian Institution.

Bent, A.C. *Life Histories of North American Shore Birds*. U.S. National Museum Bulletin No. 142, 1927. The Smithsonian Institution.

Bent, A.C. *Life Histories of North American Cardinals, Grosbeaks, Buntings, Towhees, Finches, Sparrows, and Allies*. U.S. National Museum Bulletin 237. The Smithsonian Institution.

Bent, A.C. *Life Histories of North American Warblers*. U.S. National Museum Bulletin 203. The Smithsonian Institution.

Chapman, F.M. *The Warblers of North America*. New York: Dover Publications, Inc., 1968. Republished from D. Appleton and Company 1917.

Christy, B. "The Vanishing Ivory-bill." *Audubon Magazine*. March-April 1943, pp. 99–102. The Audubon Society.

Fisher, J.; Simon N.; Vincent, J. *The Red Book – Wildlife in Danger* London: Collins, 1969.

Fyfe, R. "Bringing Back the Peregrine Falcon." *Nature Canada Magazine*. Vol. 5 No. 2, June 1976, pp. 10–17. Canadian Nature Federation.

Godfrey, W.E. "Birds of Canada." National Museum of Canada. Bulletin No. 203. Biological Series No. 73, 1966.

Greenway, J.C. Jr. *Extinct and Vanishing Birds of the World*. Second Revised Edition. New York: Dover Publications, Inc. 1967.

Hagar, J.A. "Nesting of the Hudsonian Godwit at Churchill, Manitoba." *The Living Bird*. The Laboratory of Ornithology, Cornell University, 1966, Edition 5, pp. 5–42.

Hanson, H.C. *The Giant Canada Goose*. Southern Illinois University Press, 1965.

Hewitt, C.G. *The Conservation of the Wildlife of Canada*, New York: Charles Scribner's Sons, 1921.

Hope, C.E., and Shortt, T.M. "Southward Migration of Adult Shorebirds on the West Coast of James Bay, Ontario." *The Auk*, 1944, Vol. 61, pp. 572–576.

Hubbard, J.P. "A Study of the Relationships of the Mexican and Mallard Ducks," 1976 Manuscript.

Huey, W.S. "Comparison of Female Mallard with Female New Mexican Duck." *The Auk*, Vol. 78 No. 3, July 1961, pp. 428–431.

International Union for Conservation of Nature and Natural Resources. *Red Data Book* Volume II.

Jacobs, M.H. "New Hope for the Attwater's Prairie Chicken." *The South Texas Chamber of Commerce Magazine*, April 1968, pp. 4–12.

Johnsgard, P.A. "Evolutionary Relationships Among the North American Mallard," *The Auk*, Vol. 78 No. 1, Jan. 1961, pp. 3–5.

Kuyt, E. "Whooping Cranes: The Long Road Back." *Nature Canada*, Vol. 5 No. 2, June 1976, pp. 3–8.

Lehmann, V.W. "The Attwater's Prairie Chicken, Current Status and Restoration Opportunities." *Transactions of the 33rd North American Wildlife and Natural Resources Conference*, March 11–13, 1968, pp. 398–407.

Lehmann, V.W. "Attwater's Prairie Chicken." *National Parks and Conservation Magazine*, Vol. 45 No. 9, Sept. 1971.

Lehmann, V.W., and Mauermann, R.G. "Status of Attwater's Prairie Chicken." *Journal of Wildlife Management*, Vol. 27 No. 4, October 1963, pp. 712–725.

Lehmann, V.W. "Fire in the Range of Attwater's Prairie Chicken." *Proceedings—Fourth Annual Tall Timbers Fire Ecology Conference* March 18–19, 1965, pp. 127–140.

Lehmann, V.W. *Attwater's Prairie Chicken — Its Life History and Management*. North American Fauna 57. U.S. Department of the Interior, 1941.

Mayfield, H. *The Kirtland's Warbler*. Cranbrook Institute of Science, Bloomfield Hills, Michigan, 1960.

Mayfield, H.F. Note on Kirtland's Warbler. *The Auk*, Vol. 90, 1973, p. 684.

Mayfield. H.F. "Third Dicennial Census of Kirtland's Warbler." *The Auk*, Vol. 89. 1972, pp. 263–268.

Peterson, R.T. *Proceedings of the Symposium of Endangered and Threatened Species of North America*. June 1974, Washington, pp. 158–169.

Scott, Peter *The Swans*, Michael Joseph Ltd. London, 1972.

Sibley, Fred C. *Effects of the Sespe Creek Project on the California Condor*. U.S. Department of the Interior, August, 1969.

Silverberg, Robert. *The Auk, The Dodo, and The Oryx*. 1967: Thomas Y. Crowell Company, New York.

Stobo, W.T.; McLaren, I.A. "Late-Winter Distribution of the Ipswich Sparrow." *American Birds*. Vol. 25 No. 6, pp. 941–944, December 1971.